CONFESSIONS OF AN

OVERCOMER:

FROM TRAGEDY TO TRIUMPH

ROSZIEN K. LEWIS

CONFESSIONS PUBLISHING

First Printing 2018
Editor: Amanda Pittman
Cover Design and Cover layout: Colbie Johnson
Cover Photographer: Virgil Murray

ISBN: 978-0-692-95017-3

Confessions Publishingis a subsidiary of Roszien Kay LLC, Lancaster, CA 93536
roszien@gmail.com

Table of Contents

INTRODUCTION 6

CHAPTER 1: THE FATHER WHO NEVER TOOK HIS PLACE .. 8

CHAPTER 2: THE MONSTER AT NIGHT 16

CHAPTER 3: THE LITTLE MONSTER WHO UNEXPECTEDLY CHANGED MY LIFE 19

CHAPTER 4: THE MONSTER WHO STOLE MY CHILDHOOD 23

CHAPTER 5: MY KNIGHT IN SHINING ARMOR 30

CHAPTER 6- DEPRESSION, SUICIDE, AND LOW SELF-ESTEEM 36

CHAPTER 7: MOMMY DEAREST 40

CHAPTER 8: SOPHOMORE YEAR OF PAIN 54

CHAPTER 9: THE UNEXPECTED 59

CHAPTER 10: THE PARENTS WHO GAVE ME A SECOND CHANCE 65

CHAPTER 11: AND HERE COMES PTSD 71

CHAPTER 12: THE LETTER THAT CHANGED MY LIFE 74

CHAPTER 13: MICHIGAN, HERE WE COME 77

CHAPTER 14: IN THE BEGINNING 82

CHAPTER 15: THE KNOCK THAT CHANGE THE COURSE OF MY LIFE 91

CHAPTER 16: THE GATES OF HELL BROKE OPEN 95

CHAPTER 17: MY WILDERNESS EXPERIENCE 102

CHAPTER 18: BYE BYE, MICHIGAN 116

CHAPTER 19: MY REDEEMER WAS MY PROTECTOR 121

CHAPTER 20: SEND ME LORD, AND I'LL GO 134

CHAPTER 21: WHEN DEVASTATION HITS 140

CHAPTER 22: CROSSING OVER 144

CHAPTER 23: THE JOURNEY TO OVERCOMING 148

I believed, so that you too could believe.

INTRODUCTION

I was born July 19, 1983 to a 19-year-old mother and a twenty-something-year-old father. At that time, I could only imagine my parents being filled with the same feeling of excitement and love that I had when my first baby girl was born. Maybe my mother's heart raced awaiting my arrival because she wanted a daughter. Maybe my father thought about how it would feel to press his lips against the forehead of his only daughter. Maybe they both thought about dressing me in pink dresses and pretty bows. I will never truly know how my parents felt that very moment.

I was my mother's third child and my father's second. My older brother, Darrel, was from my mother's previous relationship. My older brother Marquis, who was only a year-and-a-half older than I was, was a product of my parent's union. From my birth, both older brothers served as my protectors. Three years after my birth, my parents welcomed their last child, Jacob.

I imagine outsiders assuming that our family was picture-perfect. My parents were married with four beautiful, healthy children. Their union had managed to overcome the difficulties of life. What could come against them? What could possibly tear them apart? I'm not sure if it was the fact that my father would leave when things did not go his way, or if it had been my mother's domineering personality; whatever the case had been, their marriage did not flourish as expected.

Shortly after Jacob's birth, my parents permanently separated. Not only did my father separate from his young wife, but he also separated from his children. I cannot recall much of the life I experienced with my parents prior to their separation. I can't recall memories of my father holding me. I can't recall memories of us being a complete family. I only recall one unpleasant memory.

After my parents separated, I was haunted by a single memory of my father for twenty-five years. I remember sitting on my grandmother's porch in Los Angeles, CA as my mother combed my hair. That day, my mother told me that my father was coming to see me. I still can feel the excitement and anticipation that I felt when I waited for him. After that moment, my memory draws a blank. For years I've tried to remember my father's embrace. I've envisioned resting my head on his chest as I listened to the calmness of his heartbeat. I imagined laughing hysterically while we played peek-a-boo. Time after time, I've tried to force myself to remember what happened when he finally arrived, but I can't. I can only remember the hurt I felt that day. I can only remember experiencing jolts of pain. I remember intense feelings of emptiness and rejection.

Aside from the memory of pain, I distinctly remember the image of my father in his army uniform. I remember my father climbing into the back seat of a small car in that uniform. I've replayed that image over and over again for the majority of my life. Each time, I see the face of a little girl with a broken heart. I see the pain in her eyes. I hear her muted cries. I feel pieces of her crumbling.

CHAPTER 1: THE FATHER WHO NEVER TOOK HIS PLACE

Throughout my entire childhood and teenage years, the running theme with my father was broken promises, lies, and pain. My parents seemed to constantly remain at odds with each other. They continued to butt heads and argue. I didn't understand why. Either my father would call or I would call him. After talking to me, he would ask to speak with my mother or she would ask to speak to him. As they talked, my father would say something that agitated my mother. Maybe it was that he couldn't help her financially support us. Or maybe it was the fact that he didn't make time to see us. Whatever it was, my mother yelled into the phone before hanging up in his face.

After every slam of the phone, I knew it would be a while before I spoke to my father again. Each time this scene played out, a piece of hope was lost. It was during this time that I started to daydream about what life would be like with my father. I dreamed about how it would feel to be held by my father. I dreamed about the feeling of laying on his chest listening to his heartbeat. I would even watch other little girls with their fathers and secretly wish and dream that I was her. During that time, I wished and prayed that my father would reach out to call me.

To make my dream a reality, I initiated contact with my father by contacting his sister. My aunt Deborah and I were very close. I was closer to her than to my own father. In fact, she was the only person on my father's side of the family who kept in touch with my mother. My aunt was one of the sweetest people I had known as a child. I loved her so much. A part of me always knew I would keep in contact with my father as long as I kept in contact with her.

I recall the many fond memories that my aunt Deborah and I created. She would allow me to lay across her waterbed as I pretended I was in a boat about to sink. I was completely fascinated with everything about her—from her long nails, to her sweet voice tone, and from her furniture to her meal choices. Now as I look back, I know why I was so fascinated with her. She was the only piece of my father that I had.

My aunt was the primary person who made attempts to bridge the gap between my father and I. Anytime I would ask to call her, my mother would happily hand me her number. When I built up enough courage, I would call her to get my father's number. There were many times when she didn't know where he was or what his number was. But there were those rare occasions when she gave me his contact information.

After receiving my father's contact information, I always rushed to call him. After dialing his number, I waited excitedly for him to answer the phone. Each time, I felt butterflies in the pit of my stomach. I held my breath as I prayed he would answer. I would only resume breathing when I heard his voice on the other end or I heard the answering machine.

Although my father frequently answered the phone when I called, disappointment always followed. My father and I established a pattern of talking on the phone for hours almost every day. This pattern abruptly ended when his wife became upset or when he got into another relationship. Instead of answering the phone, my father began avoiding me. He would either rush our conversation, abruptly end the call, or avoid my call all together. In extreme but all-too-familiar cases, he would change his phone number and neglect to give me the new number.

Every time I was left without contact with my father, my spirit broke. The feeling that I was not good enough slapped me in the face.

I beat myself up with thoughts of inadequacy. I believed that I was not the daughter that he wanted. I was convinced that my father did not love me.

To make my father want me, I developed patterns that I thought would convince him that I was good enough. I started to read twice as many books as I had ever read in my life, in hopes of becoming smarter. I worked tirelessly to improve myself in every area. I ate foods my mother told me that he frequently ate. I did everything in my power to educate myself on what he liked so that whenever we spoke again, I would have a lot to talk about. I thought that studying him would help us bond more. I had myself convinced that knowing more about him would earn me his love.

My opportunity to bond with my father finally came when I was 11 years old. My father had resurfaced and expressed a desire for my brother Marquis and I to visit him in Alaska. I was ecstatic. I was not only going to be flying on an airplane, but I was also going to see him. At that time, I had not seen my father in at least 5 years. The trip to Alaska was long overdue.

As I waited for our travel day to arrive, I started to daydream again. I often caught myself sitting in class daydreaming. I daydreamed while watching TV and before going to bed. I dreamt up this elaborate plan to arrive in Alaska and make my father see that he had made a terrible mistake for years. I wanted my father to realize how much he had in fact missed me. I wanted him to realize how much he had in fact loved me. I wanted my father to vow that day he would never miss another event or day in my life. I was certain that my life would change forever.

My brother and I slept the entire flight to Alaska. At first, I was scared because I had never been on a plane without my mother before. I was also scared because I was leaving everything I knew for three entire months. At that point, I had never been away from my mother or my other siblings. This was all new to me. Luckily, I found a little comfort knowing that my brother Marquis was right there by my side. I convinced myself that everything would be okay because I had one of my protectors with me.

Upon arriving to Alaska, I was struck hard with disappointment. My father was not at the airport to pick us up. The daydreams that I had convinced myself would manifest didn't. My knight in shining armor was not waiting for me. Instead, his wife waited. I wanted to immediately get back on the plane and return home. I didn't want her there picking me up. Aside from one meeting in Los Angeles years prior, I did not know her. I wasn't comfortable with her. She was not my father. She was not a part of my daydream. I wasn't familiar with her. I wanted her to leave.

Even though I was disappointed, I didn't allow it to show. I remained quiet and respectful the entire car ride to their house. I noticed she tried to do all she could possibility do to make me feel comfortable and welcomed. No matter what she did, I still felt out of place. I wanted my father. There was nothing she could do to change that.

Several days after our arrival, my father flew back home. I can't recall where he was or why he had been away, but I was excited that he was returning home. I wanted to finally have him near. As I waited for his flight to land and for him to retrieve his luggage, a rush of emotions flooded over me. My stomach was filled with butterflies. My heart raced, beating so fast I actually thought everyone in the car could hear it. I was an emotional wreck. To calm my nerves, I daydreamed.

My imaginations preoccupied my mind until my father landed. I dreamt about my desire to be a daddy's girl finally becoming a reality. In my dream, I wrapped my arms tightly around my father's neck and vowed to never let him go. I imagined the many shopping trips we would take as we walked hand-in-hand. I imagined all of the long walks we would take in the park and down the street. I imaged him loving me once and for all. My 11-year-old mind had everything all figured out.

As I sat in the back seat of the car waiting at the airport, my life seemed as if it was going to be complete. There would be no more years of separation. There would be no more missed phone calls or unreturned messages. There would be no more lies. I would never again feel hurt or disappointed by my father. At that moment, I truly believed that nothing and no one could stand in between my relationship with my father. In that moment, I felt complete.

My daydream was interrupted as my father emerged from the crowd of travelers. At the sight of him, the butterflies in my stomach fluttered once more. I wondered whether he felt them, too. I thought about whether he would like the way my hair was braided. I wondered if he would like the outfit I was wearing. As he hobbled to the car with a cast on his leg, I held my breath for what seemed like an eternity. When he reached for the door handle, I left like jumping out of the car. In an instant, I became nervous. I didn't know what to do. I sat still. The next thing I knew, he opened the back door and peeked his head inside. He smiled at me and greeted me with a kiss. I smiled back at him nervously. I felt weird. My father got into the truck and we drove home.

Although my father spoke to me the entire ride home, I was a million miles away. To my surprise, I no longer felt excited. I didn't even want to be in his presence. The love I imagined I would feel did not exist. Instead, I felt as if a hole had taken its place. His very presence made the years of daydreaming just that—a dream. Suddenly I wanted to go home to be with my mom. Instead of being in this foreign place, I preferred my own environment. I felt like a stranger in the presence of my own father. I wanted to escape, but I couldn't. I wanted to be home, but I had to stay. I had no choice but to make the best of the trip.

As the days passed, I became comfortable. I started to bond with my two older step brothers as if I had known them my entire life. I even talked with my stepmother in an attempt to get to know her. When my father returned home from work in the evenings, I sat alongside him watching TV for hours. For the very first time in my life, I found joy being with my father. I looked forward to spending time with him. No longer did I have to daydream about being close to him;

he and I were finally creating real memories. For the first time, I felt loved by my father. I didn't want to let go. I felt free and whole. Unfortunately, this feeling of security ended abruptly.

A home that appeared to be warm and loving was actually a source of turmoil. I'm not sure if the presence of my brother and I distracted its inhabitants from their reality, or whether they had previously discussed and agreed that they would change. Whatever the case was, they were able to pretend. It wasn't until our second week in the home that everyone's true colors showed. One day after returning from Kingdom Hall with my stepmother, I watched in horror as she destroyed my stepbrother's clothing, cassette tapes, and other belongings in a fit of rage. I couldn't believe the betrayal.

After my stepmother betrayed her sons, her sons betrayed me. Because they no longer wanted me around, my brothers started to make me feel like an outcast. They purposely rode their bikes faster than me through the woods even though they knew I didn't know my way around. When my father and stepmother insisted that my brothers take me places, they would complain and resent me. They made rude remarks towards me. I felt alone and targeted more and more as the days went by. I wanted to run away, but I had nowhere to go. I wanted to tell, but I had no one to tell. I found myself crying on the inside because I didn't feel safe to cry on the outside. I felt hopeless.

My hopelessness came to an all-time high when my father realized that I took candy without permission. Unbeknownst to me, my brothers told my stepmother I alone had been stealing candy from the candy jar. They flat out lied on me. They had not only shown me where the jar was, but they too had been stealing candy. To make matters worse, my stepmother, who was already uncomfortable with the bond my father and I had formed, was eager to tell my father that I had stolen candy.

I recall the horrible day my father confronted me about stealing the candy. I remember that day like it was yesterday. To this day, my body still goes into shock at the memory. Prior to that moment, I had never seen the dark side of my father. I had never imagined its existence. That evening, my father came home. I saw fire in his eyes as he entered the front door. I remember the harsh, angry tone he lashed upon me as he placed a chair in the middle of the living room floor and told me to sit down. I had no idea what would come next. I knew deep down something was terribly wrong. What did I do? Why was I the only one sitting in the middle of the floor in that cold chair? For the life of me, I couldn't think of anything I had done wrong. I had never been a problem child; I remained on my best behavior. I sat there with chills as I wondered what had I done.

After sitting there for what seemed like an eternity, my father opened his mouth. He interrogated me about the candy. I sat there wide-eyed and frozen. My heart almost jumped out of my chest and my body was covered in chills. I couldn't believe what I was hearing. Initially, I questioned whether my ears had been deceiving me before I realized my stepbrothers had lied about me. According to their fictitious account, I had stolen the candy even though they had warned me against it. They even stated that they had told me to stop each time but I wouldn't listen. My 100-pound body sat there numb, upset, and afraid.

What my 11-year-old eyes witnessed that day was a scene out of a movie starring a deranged psychopath. My father yelled loudly, paced the floor, and pointed his finger in my face. I cried as my body shuttered. I could feel my face turning ruby red as it boiled hot. My ears started to ring. My heart felt as though it would stop from the excruciating pain. The more he yelled, the further away I felt from him. I was afraid he would hit me because of his rapid, unexpected movements. My father intimidated me as if I was his arch enemy. My father bullied me. My father had become my worst nightmare. The truth had not been told. My brothers and I all took the candy. They had showed me where the candy was. I had to face the truth: my brothers set me up.

After the interrogation, I hated everyone, my father included. My dreams were, for the first time, unobtainable. Having a close relationship with my father was more fiction than fact. At that moment,

I accepted my terrible reality. My father would remain a man who I would never truly know.

A few days after the chair incident, I called my mother and requested to come home. After that terrifying day, my twelfth birthday came and went. My father and his family were Jehovah Witnesses. They refused to celebrate or even acknowledge birthdays or holidays. There was no party. There were no gifts. There had been no singing. There had been no ice cream. There had been no cake topped with burning candles. I could not understand why my father did not recognize me. He had missed the majority of my birthdays. In my twelve-year-old mind, my father should have celebrated me. I was his only daughter. That day, my numbness intensified. I became more depressed. I had hoped and dreamed that my life would change for the better by visiting him. I had hoped he would be my knight in shining armor. My hopes faded as reality hit. It was unfair. After two weeks of trying, I returned home to the monster that struck at night.

CHAPTER 2: THE MONSTER AT NIGHT

As a small child, I looked forward to night time. I loved to snuggle up in my bed and daydream until I drifted off to sleep. Unlike most children, once I went to sleep I was completely knocked out. I slept so soundly that I would frequently wake up to soiled night clothes and bedding. No matter how hard I tried, I could not feel when I needed to use the restroom. Each morning I would wake up wet, I felt defeated. Every night, I told myself I was going to wake up to use the bathroom. However, no matter how many times I rehearsed the same encouraging line, no matter how sure I was, I would wake up wet. I was extremely disappointed with myself. I couldn't understand why in the world I was unable to get up and use the bathroom like my brothers. No matter how hard I tried to escape bed wetting, I couldn't.

Each night it seemed as though I drifted into a coma. My mother would often become upset in attempts to wake me for school. For some reason, my brother Marquis and I were both dead to the world as soon as we went to sleep. No matter how much my mother would yell, we wouldn't wake up unless she popped us. Although I tried to avoid slipping into the infamous sleep coma, I still slept sound as a rock.

One night, my sleep coma was interrupted. That night was the first time I woke up to face an unfamiliar monster. I was four years old. I felt the pressure of a large hand against the outside surface of my hand. The larger hand applied a lot of pressure as it controlled my hand. I was scared frozen. Out of nowhere, a crinkly hard thing entered in and out of my small hand. I didn't know what was going on. I couldn't understand what the foreign object was in my hand. I held my breath out of fear. I held my eyes closed tight, afraid to open them. I didn't want to risk the monster seeing me. I couldn't move. I lay there confused and scared as the crinkly hard thing pounded in and out of my hand.

The motion of the crinkly thing became faster and stronger with each stroke. After what seemed like an eternity, things changed. Finally, the motion stopped as the pressure from the larger hand instantly released off of mine. My hand thumped on the mattress.

I remained frozen. I kept my eyes closed out of fear. As soon as I built up enough courage and felt safe, I opened my eyes. I heard someone peeing in the nearby bathroom. I finally opened my eyes and glanced towards the bathroom. Standing in front of the toilet was one of my teenage male cousins. He was shirtless. He wore white underwear. Peering at him in silence, I had no idea what had just happened. I couldn't even verbalize or think about what occurred. I was too innocent to understand. My older cousin had used my small hand to masturbate.

It wasn't until years later that I revealed what the monster had done that night. My oldest brother Darrell and I were having a blast playing when I was around the age of eight or nine years old. I can't recall what we were playing, but I remember the joy I felt in my heart. I can still hear the sound of laughter. I can still feel the freedom I felt at that moment. Then suddenly, I blurted it out. My brother looked at me with wide eyes and said, "I'm telling momma."

My brother ran to my mother in the living room. I was frozen with fear. My heart started to beat fast. I felt faint. I knew I would be in trouble. I didn't understand why, but I just knew. I wanted to disappear. I couldn't remember for the life of me what I said to him, but I wished I hadn't said a single word. As I sat replaying the scene in my head, I heard my mother yell for me to come to her. I was extremely terrified because I could hear the anger in her voice. Nevertheless, I made my way to the living room as requested.

Upon walking into the living room, my mother asked me what had happened. I told her everything I could remember. I was extremely scared as I recited what had happened to me that night. My mother became upset. She yelled at me for not telling anyone. I felt a hard slap on my cheek before my mother sent me to the room. I couldn't understand why she had slapped me. I didn't do anything to make the monster do what he did. I managed to block out what happened to me until the moment when I blurted it out. As I sat in the cold, lonely room, I heard my mother arguing on the phone with someone before slamming it down.

That night was the first time in my life I had felt hate towards myself. I blamed myself for what happened. If I hadn't said anything, I wouldn't have gotten slapped. If I hadn't said anything, my mom and the person on the phone would not have argued. If only I had kept my mouth shut!

Deep down I knew keeping my mouth shut was not the solution. My mother's anger was displaced and directed towards me. Perhaps she reacted so harshly because she was faced with her own reflection. Maybe she wished she had told her parents about her molestation. Did she wish she would have told her parents about the rape she endured as a teenager which stole her virtue? Whatever the reason was, I learned that day to not be afraid to tell if another monster struck. I promised myself I would tell, no matter how afraid I felt.

CHAPTER 3: THE LITTLE MONSTER WHO UNEXPECTEDLY CHANGED MY LIFE

We called her "Mandy" for short. We were close in age. She always wore pretty dresses that I coveted. Even without occasion, her mother dressed her like a little doll. Her brown hair matched her pretty brown skin. Mandy's mother showed her the affection I craved from my own mother. She was the first friend I ever admired. I wanted to be just like her. She had everything I ever wanted. I adored her and wanted her to like me, too. I wanted to be her best friend.

One bright sunny day, we took a bath together. We pretended the bathtub was a huge pool. I recall the colored squares on the bathroom wall. I can still hear water splashing as we pretended to swim like fish. Mandy told me stories of her family living outside of California. I was amazed because, aside from a short stay in Georgia, I had never lived outside of California. To me, she had the perfect life.

After hearing her talk about the various places she lived, my memory went blank. The next memory I recall is feeling her touch me in between my legs. I was shocked. I sat there with my legs open, not saying anything. I was confused. I felt a tingling sensation and warmness. Strangely, it felt good. At the time, I did not know what she was doing, but I didn't want her to stop. I had never felt that sensation before. I continued to sit there motionless and speechless as Mandy continued to fondle me.

Several minutes later, Mandy stopped. She reached out to grab my hand. She placed my hand in between her legs. I instantly felt weird. I didn't know what to do. She must have seen the shock and discomfort on my face because she never took her hand off of my hand. She guided my hand. I couldn't believe what she had done or what I was doing. I wanted her to stop, but I also wanted her to be my friend. I had friends at school, but she was nicer to me than they were. I couldn't imagine losing her friendship. I didn't want to make her mad, so I kept my hand where she had placed it. Shortly after, I blacked out.

I don't know when or how we got out of the bath tub. All I recall next was feeling her tongue on my vagina as I lay on the floor. I was shocked by the way things felt. I didn't know why it felt so good. My heart beat fast. I was scared. I knew what was happening was wrong. I wanted to stop her, but I wanted her acceptance. I wanted nothing more than for her to be my best friend, so I laid there motionless. After laying on the cold, hard floor for several minutes, my mind went blank. After everything occurred, I never told anyone. I wanted to forget what happened. Even at the age of five, I knew what happened was terribly wrong without really knowing why. I ultimately blocked what happened out until years later.

The thoughts with Mandy resurfaced when I was in high school. I started dating a guy. Though he and I didn't have sex, whenever I would be turned on by kissing him, the memory resurfaced. I'm not sure why the memory was triggered. I didn't know how to control it, either. No matter how hard I tried to suppress the resurfaced memory, I couldn't.

It was during this time that I started to regularly watch pornography. The monster, my mother's husband, had a stack of movies that I knew about. One day as I was trying on clothes and shoes in my mother's closet, I stumbled upon them. From the title of the movies, to the location where they were hidden, I knew they were something that I was not supposed to watch. I popped one of the videos in. I couldn't believe my eyes. I knew I shouldn't continue watching, but I was extremely intrigued. Through watching a male perform oral sex on a woman, I was able to suppress memories of what Mandy had done to me for days and even months. It wasn't until years later that I understood that the spirit of perversion, lust, and homosexuality entered me through Mandy.

I hated the excitement I felt. I did not like girls. I liked boys. I wasn't attracted to females. I was attracted to males. But whenever I thought about what had happened to me or watched pornography, I became excited. As I rehearsed the thoughts and replayed the memories of Mandy that day, I started to believe the possibility that I was gay. It was at that moment that I started to hate myself more and more. I didn't want to be a lesbian. I didn't want to be with a girl.

I battled hard. I never told anyone about what I was experiencing. I was afraid that if I spoke out about my struggle, it would become true. I felt that by speaking about it, maybe I would become homosexual. To make matters worse, the regular fear of becoming homosexual led me to think about girls, to the point where I started to dream about oral sex with them. After every dream, I woke up utterly disgusted and ashamed. I couldn't understand what was wrong with me. Why couldn't I just make the thoughts go away? I was confused and scared. I felt as though my mind had betrayed me.

I started to hate the fact that I was capable of being aroused. My hatred towards myself resulted in suicidal thoughts. I didn't want to be gay, but I was excited by what I saw in the moment. I hated myself afterwards, but could not stop popping in those movies to watch the images. I was stuck in an ugly cycle that I couldn't escape. I didn't know what to do.

Suicide seemed like the logical solution at the time, until I started having sexual intercourse. The thoughts of what I was doing while having sex seemed to overshadow the thoughts of females. I was quite relieved when this occurred. I started to feel normal. I no longer felt gay, even though the thoughts crept in from time to time. My dreams and my desire to watch pornography began to drift away.

It wasn't until I surrendered my entire being to God that I was delivered. Prior to surrendering, I didn't understand why I had battled with what I had battled. I thought it would be something that would stick with me forever. I had learned to live with the unpredictable dreams and images. I felt as though they were manageable because they had become rare. As long as I was sexually satisfied by a man, they didn't exist. I was completely fine living that way.

During my breaking and molding period, God revealed to me that I battled the spirit of perversion. He even pointed to the exact point that the spirit entered me. When I was molested at four years old, I was introduced to perversion. A year later, in that bathtub with Mandy, the spirit of homosexuality entered into me. The sad reality is that before my private area had been touched by a male, I knew what it was to be touched by a female. God revealed to me that I was unable to suppress homosexual images and memories because the spirits of lust and perversion were strong in my life. I didn't possess the power to bind them up and cast them out prior to becoming saved and filled with the Holy Spirit.

Once God's power engulfed me, I no longer lost the battle. I was able to cast the thoughts out as soon as they came in. When I slept, I was able to call on the name of Jesus as soon as the enemy attempted to attack me with sexual images and feelings in my dreams. I started to experience firsthand the power of the name of Jesus. Looking back, I'm extremely grateful for the blood of Jesus. God is a true deliverer. I have been delivered from all of the foul spirits that entered into me as a young child. I could not overcome them on my own. Once I was washed by the blood of Jesus, I was able to overcome.

CHAPTER 4: THE MONSTER WHO STOLE MY CHILDHOOD

In the middle of the night, I woke up to pounding on my foot. I thought I had been dreaming, but my dreams had never felt so real before. I felt my foot covered with a slippery matter. "What the heck is going on? Why do I hear heavy breathing? Why is there panting? …what the heck is going on?" I asked myself. Then it clicked. The monster was back again. *No, no, no, no, no!* I thought to myself. This was a bad dream. How could this be? Why would he do such a thing to me?

He kept pounding my foot with his slimy penis. My body froze. My heart broke. I felt like vomiting. I was scared. With each pound, I felt my foot getting moister. I prayed that he would stop. I prayed that I was dreaming. I could hear myself scream on the inside, "God please let it be a bad dream!" I wished I had been dreaming, but I knew I wasn't.

I wanted the pounding to stop, so I shifted. My foot was in a position where he couldn't reach it. My heart started to beat faster as I waited to see what would happen next. My eleven-year-old mind turned over and over again. I still hoped this had all been a really bad dream. As the seconds passed by, I knew it hadn't been. I kept praying "God please let this be a bad, terrible, horrible dream." My heart cried, but no tears ran down my face. I laid there in silence hoping he would leave.

Instead of leaving, he continued to wait. I shifted once more hoping he would abandon his evil plans. I wanted him to flee, but he didn't. As the moments passed, I became more and more afraid. *What was next?* I had no idea how I would get out of this. Inside I screamed for help, but my mouth would not move. I was paralyzed with fear. I didn't know what he was capable of. I never thought he, out of all people, would molest me. I trusted him more than I trusted my own father. Secretly, I wished he had been my father. I admired him. I respected him. I loved him more than I loved my own father. He let me down. Instead of being my protector, he was my predator. I had unknowingly been his prey.

I shifted once more. This time, I made the mistake of extending my arm out of my bed. He waited a few seconds before placing his erect penis in my hand. Instantly, I felt four years old again. He placed his hand on the outside of my hand like my cousin had done several years prior. I could feel the same pressure being applied. The only difference was my hand wasn't as small as it had been previously. He made my hand grip his penis. I became numb. I couldn't feel my body. I no longer could hear my heart pounding. I wanted to die. I hated myself. "What could I have possibly done to deserve what was being done to me?" I asked myself. I just knew it had to be something I did. I laid there praying it would end.

Suddenly, the pace changed. I felt him move my hand up and down faster than before. Things were happening exactly as they had happened seven years prior. I felt as though I was four years old again. Unlike before, I knew the abuse would soon come to an end. I heard him breathe deeper as he pounded his erect penis with my limp hand. His hand applied much more pressure by this time. I heard a soft moan. It was over. My hand felt slimy and warm. I wanted to vomit. I continued to lay on my bed with my arm extended in fear.

I lay there still as standing water. I heard him walk to the door and slowly turn the knob. I heard the door creek as he opened it. Every movement he made seemed rehearsed and calculated. It was as if he had done it many times before. As my heart pounded, I listened in fear for his next move. I knew that I needed to make a move while I was safe. I heard him go into the bathroom directly next to my bedroom. He closed the door shut behind him.

I gathered all the strength and courage I had, and I ran. I ran past the bathroom door where the monster was. I could hear the water running. I could tell he was washing away the evidence. My heart was in my throat as I ran. I kept running until I reached my mother's bedroom door. Once at her door, I entered inside. I called her with a whisper. "Momma wake up," I said. She didn't move. I repeated this until she finally woke up. She popped her head up and said "what?" I told her as much as I could as quickly as I could. My mother jumped up out of her bed. She was horrified and angry. I could sense her disbelief. She said "what?!" again. I became scared, confused and distraught. As I spoke, hot, wet tears streamed down my face.

After listening to me, my mother hurried out of her bedroom. She walked where her boyfriend had been. While questioning him, she slapped the tar out of him. He had a stupid confused look on his face, as if he had no idea what was happening.

"What?!" he said foolishly.

My mother told him what I had told her.

"She's lying on me!" he yelled. "Roszien, why are you lying on me?" He continued audaciously.

I could not believe what I heard. This creep had the nerve to say I was lying on him! My mother continued to yell at him. By this time, my brothers started coming out of their bedroom.

The monster continued to boldly accuse me of lying. I retreated within myself. I couldn't understand what was happening. I couldn't understand why he had lied. Why would he say I was lying? *He* came into my room and used my hand and foot illegally. *He* used my body parts while I was sleeping to masturbate. It was *he* who victimized me, not the other way around! I had loved him before this moment; I had no motive to lie.

I could tell that my mother was torn. I heard her ask to see his penis. After a few seconds of them being turned away from my sight, I heard rage in her voice. His penis revealed him. Apparently, it was still red from all of the pounding he had done. He tried his hardest to convince her that he hadn't done anything. I heard ringing in my ears. I disassociated from reality as I watched my older brother Darrell chase him out of the house.

My aunt came over to comfort my mother. I heard them talking in a hushed tone as I laid in my bed. I laid in the same bed where I had been molested. I was plagued by torment as I laid there. My place of comfort was no longer comfortable. It had become cold. I tried to understand everything, but I couldn't.

The scene replayed in my mind. As the scene replayed, I started to hate my own hands and feet. With every tear I shed, I hated myself. No one explained the terms I heard. I was only eleven years old. I asked myself, "what does 'jack off' mean?" but found no answer. I lay there and wondered why he put Vaseline on my foot. As I asked myself these questions, it hit me. This had not been his first time.

I woke up many nights with a sock missing. I woke up many nights to a greasy foot or hand. Prior to that night, I never understood why. I never told anyone because I didn't know what to say. I just washed my hand or foot and went about my morning. I never expected the night monster to resurface in my life. I never thought I would be victimized again. My mother did everything she could do to protect me after finding out about the first incident, but she was sleeping with a monster. She shared a child with him. He had been her everything.

Before that night, I never understood why he and I never truly bonded. Things always seemed weird between us. But that night explained it all. He had been secretly molesting me all along. He couldn't get close to me because he had been victimizing me as I slept soundly. I hated the fact I slept so deep. Sound sleep then became a curse.

I promised myself that I would train myself to be aware of my surroundings. I intended to train myself to wake up when I heard noises. I would no longer sleep with my bedroom door open. "If only I had been more aware, this would have never happened," I thought to myself. I continued to blame myself until I saw the sun shining through my bedroom window.

For the next two weeks, there was a weird vibe in our home. No one dared to talk about that night. No one asked me how I was doing. My mother didn't allow the monster to come back even though he called a million times. Everyone seemed weird, myself included. That night my innocence was stolen. I knew my life would never be the same. I was a wreck, both mentally and emotionally. Physically, I was numb.

During this time, I didn't speak or think about home while at school. School was my safe haven. While at school, I didn't think about what happened. I also didn't speak about the monster because I was afraid. I didn't want anyone to know what happened. I didn't want to be separated from my brothers and sister. Even though I felt lonely and invisible, my siblings made me happy. We had a bond that no one could break. I couldn't see them suffer any more than what they had suffered as a result of the abuse I endured. I saw that I had caused enough problems by telling my mother; I didn't want to cause any more problems for them. My siblings were all that had.

Just when I thought I was getting to a point where I was going to be okay, I received a major blow. One day I came home from school to find the monster back. I could not believe my eyes. How could my mother let him back in? Why would she do something like that? I felt sick to my stomach. There was no possible way that she believed me. I felt disconnected from my mother from that day forward. My mother became a person I hated. At that time, I had never hated anyone. I didn't hate my older cousin who had molested me when I was four years old. I didn't even hate my detached father. But I hated my mother and the monster she loved.

To cope with living with my perpetrator, I got lost in books and school work. Whenever I didn't have anything to work on for school or books at home to read, I would go to the library to checkout more books. My teachers were impressed by how much I enjoyed reading and the knowledge I gained. Little did they know that books were my lifeline. I became energized with each story. I imagined I was the main character. The more I believed I was someone else living a different life, the less pain I felt. As long as I saw the world through their eyes, I believed there was a better day coming.

The stories in the books helped me to deal with what occurred as well as what continued to happen. That night the monster was discovered in my room was the first of many nights. Even though he had been caught, the monster continued to strike. I recall waking up to pounding on either my hand or foot, jumping up out of bed, and running to tell my mother. Each time, the monster was thrown out of the house for a few days. After the few days of exile, the monster was allowed back in the house.

The molestation continued for a few years. My mother allowed him back in the home after every episode. She even married him. I could not believe what was going on. At the wedding reception, I felt betrayed the entire time. Everyone in attendance wished them well. Everyone, including those who knew about the molestation, approved. I was the only one that felt as though their union was wrong.

The day of their reception, I was in a dark place. I was deeply wounded. I felt as though I was trapped in a prison. I screamed but my lips did not move. I cried but no tears came out. I wanted to die.

After their wedding, the molestation continued. He established a routine. The routine had been so established that I fell into a state of depression. I remained in a state of loneliness. I was hopeless. I frequently contemplated suicide. The molestation started to affect many aspects of my life. I started wearing baggy clothing to hide my body. Even though I was underdeveloped and I didn't know what he saw in me, I wore baggy clothes to be on the safe side. Prior to being molested by the monster, I didn't pay attention to male teachers. Afterwards, male teachers disgusted me. I hated having male teachers because I would stare at their pants. I didn't understand why it had become so difficult for me to look away, but I continued to. Older males disgusted me. I didn't trust men. I thought boys were attractive, but I didn't have crushes on them like my friends did. I wanted nothing to do with males.

My disinterest in guys started to fade towards the end of middle school. I actually started to desire to be in a relationship. I went from wearing oversized clothing, to skirts, fitted dresses, and fitted pants. I no longer hid underneath boy clothing. I even became co-caption of the drill team. I worked harder than most of the other girls. I danced harder and volunteered to do everything. Life had become good. I didn't have as many suicidal thoughts. The molestation wasn't as frequent (or maybe I didn't know it occurred). My grades were great. My depression, though still present, wasn't as bad. I believed there was a light at the end of the tunnel.

My hope for a better day quickly shattered. The monster started to strike again. I would wake up in the morning to find my hand or foot moist. I didn't tell my mom because she wouldn't have believed me. I thought "why would she believe me?" She wouldn't even consider it had happened without proof. When I caught him in the act, she didn't do anything besides kick him out for a few days. I washed my hand or foot in disgust while vowing to not sleep as hard as I had that night.

After many offenses, I had learned to sleep lighter. I started to jump up when I heard the slightest noise. My mother used to get extremely upset at me because I would jump up when she came into the bedroom. It drove her insane, but it gave me courage and confidence. The molestation ceased. I, for the first time, felt like I had victory over my situation.

CHAPTER 5: MY KNIGHT IN SHINING ARMOR

My feeling of victory was short-lived. One evening, after I arrived home from school, I went to sleep earlier than usual. Prior to going to sleep, I laid my younger sister in the bed with me. My mother was working. My brothers were in their bedroom. The entire house was calm and cozy. Everyone and everything was in its proper order.

On that particular night, everything seemed normal. I could hear the television playing in the background as I slept. Unexpectedly, I felt someone rubbing up against my foot. For a moment, I thought I was dreaming. I quickly realized it was the monster. Unlike the previous times, there was no Vaseline. His penis was still covered by his clothing. I jumped up and started to yell and scream at him. I was pissed off. I was enraged. My blood boiled as hot tears streamed down my face.

The monster attempted to convince me that he had done nothing wrong. He tried to convince me he was patting my sister's back to put her back to sleep. I became even more upset by the fact that he lied to my face. I ran out of my room and ran through the living room and down the hall to my brother's bedroom. I told them what had happened. We called my mother at work. As we waited for my mother to arrive home, I got in one of my brother's bed and cried. I felt hopeless. I felt shame.

The next morning, I woke up in my own bed. My older brother Darrell shook me as he called my name. He kept asking me "did that nigga do it again?" I was too embarrassed to answer his question. I was tired of the drama. I was over the shame. I was numb and felt betrayed. I told him to leave me alone as I turned over. I didn't see the point of telling him anything. I didn't want to recite the facts again. No one did anything to protect me. I was tired of telling in hopes that I would be protected only to be disappointed.

Though I didn't tell Darrell what happened, my brother Marquis did. I guess the molestation started to take a toll on him as well. Marquis called and told Darrell, who had been living elsewhere, what occurred that night. Unbeknownst to any of us, Darrell was also fed up with the molestation. After learning the details of the attempted attack, Marquis and Darrell planned to end the molestation once and for all.

It was a Saturday morning. I was at drill team practicing for the upcoming competition. My younger brother Jacob came running into the auditorium where we had been practicing. Jacob told me I had to go home with him. Judging by the tone of his voice, I knew it was serious; I got my belongings and left. Jacob told me my brothers had beaten the monster. I was happy and worried at the same time. "Finally, someone stood up for me!" I thought to myself. But I was worried because I didn't want my brothers to get in trouble. I knew my mom would raise hell—she always protected the monster.

As we walked home, Jacob told me everything. Marquis unlocked one of the doors. Darrell came into the house unannounced. Once in the house, Darrell walked up to the monster. They argued, the monster attempted to leave. Darrell swung blows at the monster. The monster ran out of the house. Once out of the house, he bolted towards his parked car in the front of the house. Because of construction work on the sidewalk, there was a huge pile of broken rocks near the car. As the monster attempted to get away from Darrell, he ran on top of the pile of crushed rocks. Darrell followed behind him and pinned him on the rocks. They continued to struggle. Darrell struck him repeatedly. Somehow the monster was able to get up and run to his car. Once at his car, he was able to get inside.

As the monster sat inside his false sense of safety, Marquis and Darrell stood on the hood of the car, stomping the windshield. They stomped the windshield forcefully and passionately. I can only image the rage they felt.

31

With each stomp, thoughts of every nighttime incident resurfaced. With each stomp, I imagined the pain they released from the betrayal that affected each one of us. With every stomp, I could imagine my very own tears being released. Each stomp represented every ounce of hurt they felt from the betrayal. With every stomp, their pain was being released.

As Jacob described to me what took place that day, I saw the monster's car driving slowly down the street. His windshield had been completely shattered in tiny pieces. I couldn't understand how in the world the windshield was still in place. He struggled to see. I saw the monster defeated, peeping through a hole in his windshield. At that moment, I felt so much peace. I was 14 years old. For at least three years, he had done the unthinkable without consequences. For years, he ruined my life. He did not care about how I had been impacted. For years he got away with his filth. For years I stood by and watched people praise him during the day while he victimized me at night. For years people supported him even though they knew there was a monster within him. For years he did good deeds in the open while destroying me in the dark. For years he thought he was invincible. Finally, it all caught up with him.

That shattered windshield represented me. I was broken in many pieces, yet still holding up. I was suicidal, yet I lived. I was depressed, yet I smiled. I hated myself, yet I loved others. I lived in constant pain, yet I cared to make my siblings happy. Just like the windshield, I was fragmented yet somehow intact.

As shattered as I had been, my siblings held me together like the outer seal of that windshield. The smiles on their faces and the happiness they exuded on a daily basis prevented me from telling outsiders about the abuse. Though I experienced so much pain, I couldn't live without seeing their smiles or hearing their laughter.

Even though I had never truly experienced love, I loved them. I even loved them more than I loved myself. They were truly the pieces that held my shattered soul intact.

When I arrived home, my mother was livid. I watched her rant and rave about what she was going to do to my brothers. She yelled numerous threats and obscenities that my mind hand difficulty keeping up. She was passionately angry. As I watched her carry on like a lunatic, I couldn't help but ask myself why hadn't she had the same passion for me. As she defended the monster, a flame of hatred was sparked within me. When he molested me, she didn't react that way. There was no "Be on the lookout." I was astonished. At that moment, I vowed to do all that I could to get out of her house. I vowed that once I left, I would never return.

The reality was that my mother cherished her relationship with the monster. She cherished that relationship more than our relationship.

With every passing second, I became even more disgusted. Another part of me died that day. I no longer felt sorry for my mother. I no longer saw her as a victim. I no longer cared about her heart.

After the fight, I became determined. I became bold. I was willing to protect myself at all costs. Routinely, I woke up in the middle of the night. I slept with knives under my mattress and pillows. I was prepared to do whatever I had to do to protect myself. If I was kicked out of the house, so be it. I refused to lay down and let anyone to put their filthy, abusive penis on me. I refused to stay silent when I knew things were wrong. No longer would I play dead.

The monster was unable to successfully strike again. As I become older, I gained new privileges. This newfound freedom allowed me to stay up longer. After reaching 16 years old, I was able to talk openly on the phone with guys. I spent many nights and early mornings on the phone. One night in particular, the monster attempted to strike. I had just finished talking to my then boyfriend. I was on cloud nine. I laid on the floor with the phone near my head. I remember hearing the shower turn on as I began drifting off to sleep. I heard someone open my bedroom door. I assumed it was my mother so I didn't jump up. I just laid there peacefully dreaming about my boo. Abruptly, I felt a soft tap on my foot. Panic set in. The tap was not accidental; it had been deliberate. I knew it was the monster even though I kept my eyes closed. My younger siblings were asleep. My mother was in the shower. There had been no one else in the house aside from us. It had to have been him.

A few seconds went by before there was any movement. I heard him move in closer. I allowed his foot to brush up against my foot once more. He was testing the waters. He was trying to see if I would move. "He has the audacity to even *try* me," I thought to myself. I regretted not being on my bed. I had no access to my knives. I wanted blood but had no weapon. Without my weapons, I jumped up and went off. The fact that he had the audacity to try to touch me sent me into a mad fury. My blood was boiling. I was intoxicated by wrath. As I yelled angrily, he yelled back lies. His eyes were huge as if he was a deer caught in head lights. I felt empowered in that moment as he stood back defending himself with lies.

"I came in to get the phone!" He yelled.

"You're lying! The phone was nowhere *near* my foot! You came to try to do that mess again!" I retorted, enflamed.

My mother heard us yelling from the shower. As I yelled back, I saw my mother coming into the room. From the look on her face, she was pissed. But I didn't care. I was pissed too! After listening to both sides, she told him to leave the room. I was confused. She even turned to me and started to fuss about her being "sick and tired of the mess." She even brought up the fact that I jump up every time she comes into my room. "Are you *serious?*" I thought in disbelief. She continued fussing about how I jump up and act as if someone is going to do something to me. All I could think was "you damn right, this nasty nigga been doing something!" I stood there unsuccessfully trying to plead my case. After her rant was over, she left.

I sat there in the dark thinking for hours. I was annoyed. I was agitated. "Here she goes again taking his side," I thought bitterly. In the midst of my emotion, I felt pleasure. I was proud of myself. I didn't play the victim. I stood my ground. I fought back and *finally* advocated for myself. A smile came across my face as I drifted off to sleep.

I had no idea my boldness would have consequences. After that night, it seemed as if the monster was out for my blood. He placed a phone recorder on the telephone. He locked the recorder in an orange heavy duty tool box. Every last one of my phone conversations were recorded and there was nothing I could do about it. Fortunately for me, the guys I spoke on the phone with were respectful.

When the phone recorder plot failed, the monster upped the ante. He tried everything in his power to turn my mother against me. He lied to my mother that I was sleeping around with guys instead of running track or cross country. I was infuriated. I was a nearly straight-A student. I was still a virgin. I wasn't ditching to have sex with boys, I was in fact running my little heart out. I wasn't even thinking about sex at that point. But my mother believed him.

My mother started to accuse me of sleeping with guys. "I know how fast ass girls are. I was once your age," she would often say. I became so offended that I wanted to fight her. I hated when she compared me to her. I was not her. My mother had become pregnant and given birth to her first child at 15 years old. I never wanted to be a young mother. I wasn't having sex. All I did was kiss, hug, and hold hands. That's all I was interested in doing. The accusations caused me to become stressed and depressed. I felt hopeless and alone. I thought my life would never get better.

CHAPTER 6- DEPRESSION, SUICIDE, AND LOW SELF-ESTEEM

I was extremely awkward during my first couple of years in high school. Boys talked about me because I was skinny with a flat butt and tiny breasts. To make matters worse, I had bad acne. My forehead spotlighted bright red pimples. As a result, my self-esteem was extremely low. I felt like an outsider. No matter how many associates and friends I had, I always felt as though I didn't fit in anywhere.

During my sophomore year, my depression and self-esteem hit an all-time low. I began having suicidal thoughts. The issues at home felt inescapable. I became sleep deprived from waking up after every sound I heard. To make matters worse, I started to compare myself to the other girls at school. My thoughts became increasingly negative. I would often think, "I'm not pretty enough like my mom and sisters." I told myself, "you're flat everywhere except for your pimply forehead." I obsessed over the fact that the other girls dressed better than me and I wasn't invited anywhere. I felt as if I was invisible when I wasn't being bullied by the boys.

I made up in my mind that I wanted out. I was convinced that the world would be a better place without me. My family would be happier without me. I was the reason for tension in the home. My childhood had been comprised of abuse, low self-esteem, suicidal thoughts, and depression. I assumed things would get better as I got older but they remained the same. In fact, things seemed to have gotten worse. My body started to affect me. I experienced frequent chest pains. At times, my physical pain was unbearable. I felt trapped and wanted out.

Then, I had to defend myself against accusations that were untrue. My mom constantly accused me of sleeping around with boys when I was still a virgin. The monster seemed to be out to get me at every turn. Things became unbearable. I felt hopeless. I was extremely lonely. I felt unloved and unlovable. I wanted out. I didn't know what method would be the most effective or how I wanted to do it. All I knew was I wanted to be done with the horror of my life.

During my season of contemplating suicide, I visited my grandparents a lot. I loved being around them because I felt peace in their presence. With them I was able to forget about all of my problems. We would spend time talking about all things positive. My grandmother talked to me about God so much that I felt as if I actually knew Him for myself. I could actually feel God's love through her. My grandmother's spirit was sweet and comforting. It was exactly what I needed at that time.

One of the rules in my grandparent's house was that you had to attend church with them. I didn't mind their rule at all because I loved the freedom I felt in church. I remember being a little girl experiencing the Holy Spirit. It was so calming and pure. It was so soft and sweet. I knew I needed that spirit. Instead of fighting against their rules, I went along with them willingly.

The more I went to church with them, the more involved I became. I even got a mentor who was young and sold out for Jesus. Her spirit was so refreshing. She dressed so fashionably and modestly. Her hair was always neat and well-kept. She was a representation of the woman I wanted to be. I admired and loved her zeal for Christ so much that I helped her with whatever she needed help with.

During this time, I got involved. I helped with the children's ministry. I was on the praise dance team. I sang in the youth choir even though I couldn't hold a note. I became a part of the purity club. I participated in church plays. I went all in. Church had become my new coping skill. It had replaced my obsession with books and daydreaming.

Though I did all of these things, I remained suicidal. The problem was that when I left church I still had to face the demons at home. It seemed as if the more I pressed in and did more for church, the more my demons weighed heavy on me. My state of depression had been like nothing I had experienced before. I started to lose weight. I stood 5'4 and weighed a good 100 pounds. My negative thoughts intensified. They seemed to never leave. Suicide became my only option at that point.

The day I reached my all-time low, I went to church out of routine. My only intention that day was to get through church, then go home to decide how and when I would commit suicide. I forgot it was youth Sunday that day. Had I remembered, I would have skipped church all together. I almost didn't go to church because of how broken and hopeless I felt. But for some reason, I mustered up enough strength to go.

When I arrived, my mentor asked me to help her lead testimony service. "Oh Lord," I thought. I quickly declined. As far as I was concerned, I had absolutely nothing to testify about. I wanted to die as quickly as possible. I had made up my mind that I would commit suicide. I was weak in my body. I felt crazy because I couldn't control the thoughts in my mind. I was like a walking zombie. What did I possibly have to thank God about? The more I resisted, the harder my mentor pushed. Finally, I gave in. I agreed to lead the service with her.

As I stood at the front of the church facing the congregation, I crumbled inside. I felt as if I had already died. I wanted the moment to end. I could hear my mentor speaking, but it sounded as if she was a million miles away. Next, I heard the congregation singing. I could hear my own voice singing but I sounded as if I, too, was a million miles away. I couldn't even feel my lips moving. After what seemed like an eternity, the congregation stopped singing. It was now my turn to testify. I felt my heart racing for the first time in a while. I opened my mouth to testify. I heard myself recite the words that I had heard every Sunday during testimony service, "I thank God." Before the words could escape my mouth, I felt something rise up in the pit of my belly. I felt as if there was a war going on in my belly. I felt pulling. The spirit of suicide fought violently to stay inside of me. I had no control over the struggle happening inside of my body. I yelled and cried as I bent over, attempting to gain control.

I was beyond scared. I didn't understand what was happening to me. My tears fell like streams of water. The entire time I heard my grandmother in my ear yelling, "say thank you Jesus, thank you Jesus. Put ya hands up. Say thank you Jesus, thank you Jesus." I struggled to speak. My body moved from one side of the church to the next. All the while, my grandmother and her crew surrounded me and prayed. The more the struggle continued, my grandmother continued to yell, "say thank ya Jesus, thank ya Jesus." I said as much as I could through the screams gushing out of my belly. I heard myself moaning and screaming. I was boiling hot. I could feel a war going on inside of me. I didn't fully understand what was going on, but I knew it was necessary. I felt as though this war lasted for an eternity.

Suddenly, the war ceased. Once it stopped, I felt completely cleansed from head to toe. It was as if my spirit had been washed and cleansed. I no longer felt the heaviness of depression or suicide. I no longer felt numb. I no longer felt like a stranger in my own body. I felt lighter. I felt different—a good different.

That morning was the last morning I experienced suicidal thoughts. When I left church that day, I was renewed in my spirit and my mind. I was born again. It was as if God had performed surgery on me. When he had finished operating, he threw away the evil spirits of suicide and low self-esteem. That moment signified a turning point in my life.

I no longer battled with low self-esteem, depression, or suicide in high school. My acne went away almost overnight. I started to eat again. My hair started to grow more. My body started to fill out in all of the right places. I continued running track and cross country. I started working. For the first time, I had a life of my own. For the first time in my life, things were going well. A little too well.

CHAPTER 7: MOMMY DEAREST

Things were going so well in my life that I missed signs. My mother was headed down a road of destruction, and I did not even know it. My mother was being sexually harassed at work by her direct supervisor. I overheard her talking about it to other members of my family, but didn't really pay her too much mind. I didn't know at the time the impact it had on her. I had no idea her body was riddled with pain from the fear of being unexpectedly fondled or pushed into a bathroom and kissed again. I didn't know my mother started to suffer high levels of anxiety. I didn't know my mother had slipped into a deep, dark state of depression. I knew things were going on, but I failed to grasp the seriousness of it all.

At the time, I was totally engulfed in what I had going on in my own life. I was running track and cross country. I was active in different extracurricular clubs at school. I was dating someone and was experiencing "puppy love" for the first time. My thoughts were on making sure my grades were the best they could be so that I could go to college. My mind was centered on working on weekends to purchase my own clothes. I wasn't concerned about my family.

The first sign that something was wrong appeared one weekend. That Saturday, I had taken my three younger siblings to the mall and the movies. At that time, I was around 16 years old. That day, we walked into the house to hear my mother and the monster arguing upstairs. From what I gathered, they were arguing about me. My first thought was, "here we go again with the lies." By then I had become accustom to the tactics the monster used to try to keep my mother and I at odds with each other. I braced myself as we walked up the stairs. A cloud of dread surrounded me. With each step I took, I heard more and more.

As I approached the top of the stairs, I heard enough to understand why they had been arguing. I was appalled. I was shocked. All I could think was "the audacity of him!" I felt my blood boiling hot, but I contained myself. No matter how I felt, I couldn't allow him to see me sweat. I couldn't give in. I couldn't act out because it would only add fuel to the fire. So, I kept quiet as we entered. They had been arguing so intensely they didn't notice we were home.

When they realized we were home, the arguing simmered down. It was too late, though. I heard everything. I was pissed. I didn't know what to say or think. I went into our kitchen nook and sat down and cried. I was a good student. I was an obedient child. No matter how much good I did, it seemed to never be good enough. As I cried, my mother walked in and sat on the side of me. She put her arm around me. To my surprise, instead of questioning me about the accusations, she just sat there comforting me. I was surprised. As sweet as the gesture was, I was confused. After a brief moment, my mother started to speak. She told me that she knew I had been at the movies as I had stated and not at a hotel having sex as the monster stated.

I sat there astonished. For the first time, she believed me over him. I told my mother I didn't know why the monster kept messing with me. I really couldn't understand why he continued to lie about me. My mother looked into my eyes and said told me she knew how I felt and believed me. She even said she believed that he had molested me. I was stunned. For years I thought she hadn't believed me when in fact she had. She continued to speak. She told me there were some things going on and things would change. At that time she didn't mention what those things were. I sat there shocked in disbelief. I felt as if I was dreaming but knew I wasn't. I didn't know how to feel or what to say. I didn't say anything.

My mother and I sat side-by-side in silence. Deep down, I knew there was something different. When I looked into her eyes, I could tell. I just didn't know what it was. I couldn't place my finger on it. Her eyes appeared glossy. I had never seen her eyes like that before. Instead of troubling my mind trying to figure it out, I attributed the glossiness to her crying. I thought maybe she had been crying a lot because her body was relaxed like mine had been when I cried a lot.

Little did I know, my mother's composure had nothing to do with crying. My mother was high. I don't recall how I found out, but I found out. My mother was smoking crack cocaine. I imagine I was shocked, emotional, and disappointed. I imagine I cried when I found out. Maybe the shock sent my body into something. I'm not sure. All I know is that its impact caused me to black out those moments.

The reality was that my mother was a crack head. I was introduced to the smell of crack cocaine after I found out about her addiction. Prior to that moment, my mother hid it really well from us. Maybe she smoked in the car or the bathroom. Maybe she masked the smell of it. Whatever she did to conceal her drug use, she no longer felt she had to hide it. My mother smoked anywhere from that point on. There was no way for us to get away from the smell of crack while we were home. There was absolutely nothing we could do about it, either.

My mother sat around us as she smoked crack cocaine. I recall one day sitting at the computer in our dining room. My younger siblings were there as well. As I typed my English paper, my mother sat near me smoking crack and talking her head off. I will never forget the sound she made when she inhaled. It almost sounded as if she was trying to force something through a straw's small opening. I remember the sound it made when the flame touched the tip of the pipe. It sounded as if the crack rock was engulfed. I hated every second of it. But I endured.

My mother was spending time with us. She wasn't in the other room in her bed as she had done before. She wasn't riding around town with the monster. She wasn't at work busting her butt. She was at home with us, as we had always wanted. We were in her presence and didn't care what she was doing as long as she was there with us.

Due to the stress of being sexually harassed and her reporting it, my mother was on leave from work. My mother's anxiety had increased to an unbearable level because the sexual harassment had reached an all-time high. My mother frequently rushed to the hospital because she was fearful that she had been having a heart attack. Her chest would be riddled with pain and her body would experience other symptoms (this was all prior to her smoking crack cocaine). As result, my mother's doctor forced her to go on medical leave.

It was during my mother's stay at home on medical leave that she started to smoke crack. Her personality bubbled over. She had a lot of energy to keep up with us. She had the patience to spend time with us for a change. I know how crazy everything sounds, but I desired to be close to my mother. I had always wanted to spend time with her. I loved my mother despite everything, and enjoyed her company. I know I could have walked away when she would smoke, but I didn't. I just wanted to be close to her no matter what, even if it meant me being uncomfortable.

What I failed to realize at that moment was my mother's journey was going to get a lot worse. I had no idea at the time how my mother's addiction would impact our family. I had no clue that her addiction would push her away from us. I didn't realize the truth until my uncle, also a crack head, moved into our home. It was at that time my mother's addiction went from bad to worse. Prior to my uncle moving in, my mother kept everything together. Her weight didn't indicate she was smoking crack. My mother still looked like her normal self. However, once my uncle moved in all hell broke loose.

My mother's crack habit increased. My mother became extremely paranoid. She was convinced her supervisor was driving by our house at all hours of the day and night. I would catch her peeping out of the blinds in fear. She often hid as she looked out of the blinds. As I watched her, I felt as if a horror film had been unfolding before my very eyes.

One day my mother started talking about bugs crawling out of her skin. She had somehow become convinced that our pet birdbrought an infestation into our home. I watched my mother pick at her skin. I even watched her pick at her scalp for hours. My mother picked and scratched so much that she started to lose her hair. She squirmed and screamed, believing that bugs were crawling out of her skin. No matter how much she would pick the bugs out of her scalp or her skin and hold her hand up and show me, I never saw anything. I initially laughed my mother's insane behavior off. I couldn't believe what was happening. I didn't take her paranoia seriously until her paranoia started to directly affect the entire household.

As a result of my mother and uncle's paranoia and delusions, they placed insect bombs in our home. Initially, the bombs were placed in our kitchen nook where the bird spent a lot of its time. However, when the infestation did not disappear, more rooms in the home were bombed. As a result, my siblings and my belongings were shifted from room to room. It felt as though we were being displaced. I was horrified.

The smell of crack and insect bombs were the continual aroma in our home. My mother and uncle smoked crack day and night. My mother spent less and less time with us. I was utterly disgusted. I felt as though I was living in a nightmare where being outside the house was my only escape. School and work became my safe places. I became more involved in school during that time so that I wouldn't have to be home, and I continued to work on the weekends.

I became more determined than ever to get as far away from home as possible.

My determination quickly turned into desperation. One evening, I returned home from school with directives from my mother that I needed to pack some clothes. I was confused and immediately asked, "why?" My mother explained we had to check into a hotel. She said the bugs had gotten so bad that we needed to bomb the entire house. I was confused because only the crack heads saw the bugs. Nevertheless, we spent a few nights at a hotel.

With every day that passed by, my home life became even more bizarre. The sound of running water had became commonplace because my mother developed a fascination with it. My mother lived in the mirror. When I would go to use the bathroom, there she was picking her scalp. Seeing her little bald head was all too familiar. It was to the point that we would just use the bathroom with her in the mirror.

During this time, my home life made me push harder to secure a future. I managed to keep my grades up. As a result, I got accepted into every California state university that I had applied to. I decided I would go to San Diego State University. Its reputation for education was great. It was the perfect school for me. I finally started to see the light at the end of the tunnel as graduation neared.

I had anticipated my graduation day for many years. It had finally come. I was thrilled! I was closing one chapter and moving on to another chapter. The best day of my life had finally come. I was proud of myself; I made it through! During high school, I overcame suicidal ideation. I overcame depression. I overcame low self-esteem. I had managed, by the grace of God, to keep my grades up. I survived my awkward stage and had blossomed into a beautiful butterfly.

I envisioned my graduation day would be perfect. It seemed as though everything would fall into place as planned. My expectations were shattered when I took one look at my mother. She had been smoking crack for days. She was frail. She looked just like a crack head. Anyone in their right mind would look at her and know she was a drug addict. I didn't want what I saw, but I had no other choice but to accept it. I wished I could skip the graduation pictures but I couldn't. I managed to get through the interdiction without breaking down.

After graduation, I went to grad night with my classmates. I had such a blast. I was able to temporarily get past the pain I felt at graduation. I felt so free, floating on cloud nine. I felt accomplished and on top of the world. I wanted to stay in that place forever.

Unfortunately, grad night came to an end and I had to face reality. As I got off of the school bus, I didn't see my mother. Had she forgotten she had to pick me up? How would I get home? I was tired. I sat on the curb waiting for what seemed like an eternity until she finally came. I was upset at my mother. When I got in the car, she explained to me she didn't have the money for gas until she called around and got it. "Well, if you weren't smoking crack you wouldn't have this problem," I thought angrily to myself. Though I was upset, I held my tongue. My mother was no-nonsense without crack. With crack, she was insane.

As I waited to go to college, I worked, shopped, and stayed focused. I often found myself daydreaming about checking into my dorm room. I wondered how things would be. I hoped and prayed my roommate was nice. I couldn't wait to be on my own. No longer would I have to face my reality. Once I was away, I could create my own life. I could leave the life that was born to me behind. I could finally be normal and happy. I could be me with no apologies.

When the day came for me to move away to college, I was super excited. I had survived the summer. I managed to get everything I needed to take to college. My mother, younger brother Jacob, and baby brother accompanied me on the drive to San Diego. That day, SDSU's campus was full of families, eager freshman, and returning students. There I was with my family.

We hauled my belongings up one flight of stairs to my dorm room at the end of the hall. My roommate and her parents were also there. I was so thrilled that I could barely contain myself. I was *actually* moving into my dorm room! I was *actually* a college student! I could hardly believe it. If I had not been so busy hauling my belongings in, I would have pinched myself. I was normal. For an instant, I had no memories of my mother's drug addiction. I had no memories of my broken past or broken family. I was a normal freshman.

The feeling of being normal quickly faded. My false-sense-of-reality bubble was busted. As soon as we were done unloading the last of my belongings, my mother told me she was driving back home. "Wait a minute," I thought. "How could she just drop me off without helping me to get settled in? How could she not help me unpack?" I couldn't understand what was more important than helping me get settled in. Why would she miss the opportunity to help me get settled in? The other parents helped their children. I instantly felt sad, alone, and numb. I felt kicked to the curb like a pile of trash.

There was no way I would be able to change my mother's mind. She had always been the type who didn't change her mind once it was made. Instead of saying anything, I keep quiet. I felt disregarded and unimportant. This was one of the most important days of my life and I expected more support from her. I expected her to *be there*.

My first year in college was exciting. I made a lot of friends. I had managed to learn my surroundings. I got an on-campus job to make extra money because I didn't have any financial support from my family. After paying for tuition, books, and room and board, I barely had anything left from my financial aid. I, unlike most students, had to work to survive.

During this time, I kept limited contact with my family. Even though I had been off living my life, I needed to know my siblings were okay. They were still in the home with my mother and as expected, things didn't look so good. It was as if after leaving, things with my family went from bad to worse. My mother and uncle smoked more and more crack. My siblings worried constantly about whether they would have food to eat. My mother and uncle had friends around that also smoked. My siblings were exposed to so much without anyone to shield or protect them—not even the monster. He had been serving a short jail sentence.

With the escalation of dysfunction in my family and my mother's drug addiction, I worried often. I constantly thought about whether they had been eating. I had wished I could do something to help, but I was barely making it myself during this time. I did the only thing I could do, which was to pray.

I prayed until I was reunited with them for Christmas break. I was excited to be going home even though I knew what the environment would be like. I missed my family a lot. Even though I knew my mother was in a dangerous state, I went home.

Before I arrived home, my brother Marquis was released from prison. It had been at least four years since I had seen my brother. Marquis had gotten into trouble and was sent to Youth Authority. I was thrilled to finally see him in person. I knew no matter what happened, I would be able to get through it because he would be there, right by my side.

My family wasn't the only reason I had been looking forward to going home. My then boyfriend Haven would be there. Haven and I met the summer before I went to college. We carried on a long-distance relationship. Seeing and spending time with each other was long overdue.

Once I arrived home, things weren't as bad as I thought they would be. There weren't many people going in and out of the house as I had imagined. There was food in the house. And, my mother and uncle remained in one area as they smoked their drugs. I was a little relieved. This relief was interrupted the night I decided to have a heart-to-heart conversation with my mother.

That night, Marquis and I sat in the room with her. We had decided that we would talk to my mother to gain clarity. I wanted to understand why my mother allowed the monster to do what he had done to me. I wanted to know why she didn't do anything to protect me. I wanted to know why hadn't she stuck up for me. Marquis and I both assumed we would get closure from the answers she would provide. We didn't take into account the possibility that my mother would not answer our questions.

That night, I gathered all the strength and courage I had and started asking questions. The first question I remember asking her was, "momma, why?" Instead of answering the question, my mother said "I've moved on with my life. You need to move on too. I'm going to be with who I want to be with." I was crushed. All of the hope I had in my body for reconciliation and closure disappeared. How could she be so hurtful? How could she be so selfish to not want to give me what I needed to move on? I cried hard. Marquis told me it was going to be okay. I could tell from the tone of his voice he was hurt too. His voice shook with each word. It was as if he was trying to be strong for me because he knew I was crushed.

After I gained my composure, I called Haven to pick me up. He could hear the hurt in my voice even though I tried to mask it. He came over immediately. I retrieved all my belongings I had brought with me. That night, I cried myself to sleep as he held me. All of the suppressed hate I experienced towards her resurfaced with intensity. I decided I wanted nothing to do with her.

I stayed with Haven until it was time to return to school. Though my break had not turned out how I had expected, I was happy. I was happy to see my siblings. I was able to experience what I had experienced. The hurt I had felt from that trip turned into motivation to work harder. I was determined to achieve my goals even more after that trip. I had no other choice but to succeed.

The hurt I felt from my Christmas vacation trip disappeared as the school year ended. I still preferred to not live in my mother's house, but I had no choice. As the semester neared an end, I called my mother to arrange for her to pick me up. Instead of hearing her voice on the other end of the phone, I heard the voice of the operator. The phone had been disconnected. I didn't try to contact my family after I left. I didn't know how long the phone had been off. I convinced myself I had dialed the wrong number. I had to have dialed the wrong number.

I tried dialing my home number again. The same recording played, "I'm sorry you've reached a number that's been disconnect..." I couldn't accept it. I tried calling several more times. With each attempt, I was more careful to dial each digit correctly. I needed to make sure I wasn't making a mistake before I crumbed in a puddle of tears. No matter how careful I had been, the operator's voice was the only voice on the other end. Dang, the phone was disconnected. Thoughts started to flood my mind all at once. How was I going to get home? What happened? What in the world was going on? My questions went unanswered. I had no idea what to do.

I sat in the phone booth for a few minutes. After sitting there, I called my maternal grandmother. As the phone rang, I could feel my heart beat fast. I was nervous. I didn't know what I would find out. I knew something was odd. We never had our phone disconnected.

My thoughts were interrupted by my aunty Lolo's voice. I immediately asked to speak with my grandmother. For whatever reason, aunty Lolo stayed on the phone instead. I asked her had she spoken to my mother. I told her I had been calling my mother but the phone was disconnected. "Your momma got evicted," she blurted out. All I could think was, "what? she got evicted?"

After that, my aunt's voice sounded a million miles away. I blacked out for the remainder of the conversation. When I came to, I was still holding the phone receiver. I put the receiver back in its place and sat in the phone booth. I cried. I had no idea what I was going to do, and I was afraid of what was next. I was going to be homeless without a clue where to go. I sat in the phone booth for what seemed like an eternity before going upstairs to my dorm room.

As soon as I entered my bedroom, I broke down crying. My roommate was initially startled. She couldn't understand what had happened to me. I didn't know what to do but to cry. As I cried, I reached for the phone. I called the only person who had provided me with comfort that year—Haven. When he picked up the phone, I told him everything. I don't even think I stopped to take a breath. After I stopped talking, Haven told me he would call me back.

Haven knew my situation. He listened to my ramblings on many occasions and encouraged me to keep going. He had truly loved me despite my brokenness. After several minutes, he called me back. Haven told me I could live with him. I asked him if he was sure. He said, "Yes. After I told my mom everything, she said it was okay." I was shocked. At that time, I had no desire to live with a man. Don't get me wrong, I was madly in love with him. An hour couldn't go by without me hearing his voice. I just didn't want to mimic what I saw growing up.

I was grateful I had a place to live. Haven and his mother had been beyond kind and generous by opening their home up to me. There was only one obstacle that stood in my way: How was I going to get to his house with all of my belongings on such short notice? Who would drive me from San Diego to Lancaster? After searching my mind, I called the one person I could think of, my best friend Nikki.

Nikki had been one of the first people I met during college orientation. She was one of the kindest people I had ever met. She never complained about being the only person who drove everywhere. When I told Nikki all that had occurred, she was more than willing to drive me where I needed to be. I didn't even need to ask her; she just offered to help out. I was overjoyed! Everything worked out better than I imagined. I realized in that moment that Nikki was a true friend. I realized I was not alone. I realized there were people who would love, protect, and accept me though we weren't blood related.

Check-out day quickly approached. Nikki loaded her purple Nissan Sentra with her items before coming to my dorm room. When she arrived, I was worried. Her small car was already halfway filled. I didn't know if I would have to leave some of my belongings behind. I didn't have much, but what I had were the only possessions I owned. After adjusting and readjusting items, we were able to fit all of our belongings in. I was relieved. By the grace of God, everything worked out. Not only did I not have to be homeless, but I would also have all of my possessions with me.

The drive to Lancaster was smooth. On the way, I contemplated all the possibilities that lay ahead. I was nervous and excited at the same time. I was officially disconnected from the umbilical cord. I hoped and prayed for the best. I prayed I could find a job to support myself. I was grateful Haven and his mother opened their home to me, but I wanted to do all that I could to avoid burdening them.

After arriving to Lancaster, I hit the ground running. I was determined to get a job. Haven drove me around from place to place to put in job applications. I was optimistic that someone would call me. I already had a good job resume because I had worked from the age of 16. I wasn't anticipating I would have a hard time finding employment, but I did. That summer no one called me back. I felt defeated. How could a person not be hired when they had a willingness to work? This question went through my mind several times a day. I couldn't understand it for the life of me.

Although I did not work that summer, I was well taken-care-of. Haven's mother always made sure there was more than enough food in the house for us. She also made sure Haven had money. She never made me feel like a burden, nor did she ever complain about my inability to find a job. That summer, I lived in the comfort and peace that I only dreamed about. I felt loved and appreciated. I felt wanted and celebrated. I felt like family though we didn't share an ounce of blood. I felt at home.

I was included in all of their family events that summer. His mother took us to Vegas and provided us with spending money so that we could enjoy ourselves. She took us to nice restaurants. She introduced me to different foods I had never heard of. We went to family events and parties. I was beyond grateful for the memories we created. They were heroes I had never imaged I would encounter.

That summer I had minimal interaction and contact with my own family. Honestly, I didn't want to see them. Seeing them would remind me of the turmoil I come from. Seeing them would remind me of the demons from my past. I *needed* the peace and security that I experienced in Haven's home. I needed to feel loved and protected. I needed to be cared for. To see my family meant I would have to face my reality. I had grown tired of reliving the tragedies of my life. I wanted to be normal for a change. I didn't want to worry about my siblings. I couldn't help them. I definitely didn't want to think about or see my mother.

When summer was over, I returned back to school. To ensure I would never face being homeless or having to live with anyone else again, I moved into an apartment with one of my friends. At the time, I was 19 years old. I was excited and determined to provide a secure life for myself. Though my living situation had changed, I still worried about my siblings until my grandmother finally got them.

CHAPTER 8: SOPHOMORE YEAR OF PAIN

My sophomore year of college got off to a great start. I had an apartment, I worked two part-time jobs, and I was going to more events and meeting more people. My siblings were happy and flourishing despite the absence of my mother. It seemed as if my troubled days were behind me. That was far from the truth.

The first area I started to experience trouble was in my relationship with Haven. As I stepped out and enjoyed being a college student, Haven became paranoid that I was cheating on him. He wasn't fond of me going out so much with my friends. We started to argue more and more. I wanted to party and hang out with my friends. I didn't want to say home and talk on the phone anymore. I became frustrated with Haven. When he wanted to go out with his friends, I didn't mind. I wanted him to enjoy himself. I trusted him. I had no doubt in my mind about him. He, on the other hand, had grown suspicious. His distrust may have been because of the things I told him my friends had done. It may have been because of the things he himself had been doing. Whatever the case had been, there was a lot of friction.

As our arguments increased, they also escalated. Instead of there being simple disagreements, there were full out arguments. Haven even cursed me out and threatened to breakup with me on many occasions. We even started a cycle where I would go out, we would breakup, get back together, and then argue more. Initially I would get distraught, cry, and become depressed. However, the more the cycle went on, I started to distance myself from him until I finally ended the relationship.

I didn't want to continue the cycle I saw growing up. I refused to stay in a relationship where we disrespected each other. We loved each other hard, but we fought even harder. Maybe the distance had been getting to us. Maybe I started to see singleness as more desirable. Whatever the case had been, we grew apart. It was over. Neither one of us knew how to salvage things. Neither one of us wanted to be wrong. Our pride worked against us, and we didn't talk for years after the breakup.

With the breakup, I found freedom. I didn't go through the stages of grief after breakup. I almost immediately started dating again. In fact, I dated a lot. Prior to being in a relationship with Haven, I had only dated a few guys. There was a lot I needed to learn. I really didn't know what I liked or didn't like. So, I took my newfound singleness as an opportunity to explore. I learned a lot about myself and guys during that period. I learned to be happy in that season, until I started to experience unusual pain in my body.

One day, out of what seemed like nowhere, my lower back bothered me. Initially I assumed I had picked something up the wrong way at work or I had slept poorly the night before, so I brushed it off. I thought the pain would go away in a few days. However, as the days flew by, the pain intensified. As the pain intensified, I assumed that maybe I had danced a little too much the weekends prior. I didn't imagine that something more serious could be at hand. At that time, I continued to go about life as usual, expecting the pain would subside on its own.

As the weeks went by, the pain intensified greatly. I was in so much pain at night that I started to sleep in a ball. During this time I lost my appetite. I felt tremendously weak all the time. Despite the signs that something was seriously wrong, I didn't go to the doctor. Instead, I continued to push myself to work and attend class. I was young and in good health; I assumed the pain would go away and everything would go back to usual.

One morning, my denial quickly faded. I woke up and could barely move without feeling sharp pains in my lower back. My head was pounding. I felt nauseous. I knew something was terribly wrong. Growing up, I experienced reoccurring urinary tract infections. The symptoms I experienced felt as though I had a horrible infection. I knew I had no other choice but to go to the doctor's office to get antibiotics.

I mustered up all the strength I had and went to the doctor's office. I was concerned and awfully scared. As I waited for the test results to come in, I couldn't help but panic. I neglected to go to the doctor while I had mild symptoms. Whatever was wrong could have been taken care of sooner. Now, there was something *really* wrong with me. I sat there blaming myself for being so irresponsible. I had no logical reason to not go to the doctor sooner. I spent a lot of time on campus; the health center was near my jobs, and I walked past it often. I sat there that day in pain. I waited, and worried the entire time while I waited. I prayed that whatever was wrong with me wouldn't kill me or affect me permanently.

After what seemed like an eternity, my test results arrived. The doctor hurried in the room with my chart in his hand. I studied his face for signs of concern. As I looked, I became afraid. He smiled as an attempt to mask his concern. I knew what he had to say wasn't good. After smiling, he told me that both of my kidneys were infected and I was severely dehydrated. He told me the infection had gotten so bad that had I not come in that day, I would have needed to be hospitalized.

I was worried, yet relieved. If I had been hospitalized, I would have incurred hospital bills. Aside from the coverage offered through my school, I had no outside health insurance. I was glad I had finally gone to the doctor's office when I did. I was puzzled, because though I had several bladder infections in the past, I had never gotten a kidney infection. The doctor assured me I had nothing to worry about because with the medication and adequate rest, I would be back to normal in no time. I was relieved knowing that I didn't cause permanent harm to myself.

As I sat in the waiting area of the health center, I couldn't help but to try to make sense of everything. The more I tried, the more bizarre things seemed. I was a million miles away. I could feel the solution going into my blood stream to help hydrate me. I could feel the pain letting up as the pain medication kicked in. "I almost caused myself to be hospitalized because I didn't listen to my body," I thought to myself.

As soon as the solution from the IV had completely finished, I was sent home. I was tired. Aside from the prescribed medication, I had nothing else to comfort me. There was no one I could call. I had no one to help take care of me. All of those close to me had a demanding life. I had no family near, no mother or father to call. I had no one to come to my rescue. I was all I had.

During the time I had been sick, I missed school and work. I had no energy to do anything besides sleep in a ball. I grew lonely. My body was riddled with pain until the infection was lifted. The pain medication helped but wasn't a complete solution. As I laid there in my dark, cold room, I prayed I would never feel what I felt again. The pain and the loneliness was too much to bear.

The infection lifted about a week later. By that time, I was ready to get back in the groove of things. I had to somehow catch up on my class assignments. I had no idea how I would manage to fit more reading into my schedule. I needed to work, so missing more work was out of the question. I didn't know what to do. I knew I needed to do it all somehow, so I pushed myself to do everything.

A little while after the first kidney infection, my body was hit with another kidney infection. Instead of waiting until the pain became unbearable, I went to the doctor right way. Again, I received medication and an order by the doctor to rest. I had already missed a lot of school and work. I couldn't afford to miss work because I needed money to care for myself. I refused to be homeless. I also didn't want my hours cut, or even worse—to be fired. Against the doctor's orders I continued to work. Every day, I forced myself to report to work as scheduled. I had to gather all the strength I had. It was extremely difficult. I was miserable. I experienced intense pain. I wanted to fall apart on many occasions but couldn't. I had no choice but to push myself until the infection cleared.

Once the second kidney infection cleared, I went back to class. Because I hadn't gone to class the week I had the second kidney infection, I was even more behind. I kept telling myself I could do it and I pushed through. I even started to see the light at the end of the tunnel. Everything in my life started to stabilize. My health was better. School was going well. And my family seemed to be doing well, too. I was enjoying life again.

CHAPTER 9: THE UNEXPECTED

One day, I received a phone call from my brother Marquis. Marquis told me the monster had been released from jail. "Ugh…" I began to think. My thoughts were interrupted by Marquis' voice. He said, "he's in a wheelchair." I couldn't believe my ears. Honestly, I was happy. I felt as though God was repaying him for the years of torture he inflicted on me. Marquis continued to speak. He told me the monster had been diagnosed with prostate cancer and was wheelchair-bound.

I had absolutely no sympathy for the monster. Marquis told me my mom was sad. I expected her to be. I didn't care at all about how anyone felt. I felt as though he was being punished for the nasty things he had done. He deserved every ounce of pain and every cancer cell. He deserved it for all the lies and the years of molestation. He deserved to feel pain because I had felt pain.

As I sat on my lunch break days later, I received a call from my mother. My mother and I talked briefly before she told me the monster wanted to talk to me. "Oh, Lord what does he want?" I thought sullenly. I had absolutely nothing to say to him. We had nothing to talk about. I had years of bitterness bottled up inside of me which I was ready to release. Before I could say no, the monster began to speak.

He apologized for everything he had done all those years. He said, "I'm sorry for what I did to you. Sometimes the devil gets in us and has us doing things." As I listened, I was conflicted. On the one hand, I couldn't believe he had actually admitted to what he had done. On the other hand, I was annoyed because he was shifting the blame to the devil. With these conflicting thoughts, I was shocked and speechless. I never imagined he would admit what he did because he lied for so many years. I didn't know how to feel. I became numb. Through the numbness and disbelief, I heard myself say, "it's okay." Even though the apology took years to come, I had no choice but to accept it. It pushed me a little closer to closure.

The monster passed away later that year. He passed away in a hotel room with my mother and baby brother watching. I thought I wouldn't feel anything, but I did. I actually felt bad. I cried along with everyone else at his funeral. My mom cried a lot that day. When I thought about the fact that she was a widow at the tender age of 38, my heart broke for her.

My mother stood by her husband's side until death. She had taken care of him. He passed away in her arms. Even though the cancer spread rapidly throughout his body, he was at peace. Prior to him passing, he made peace with God. Not only did he start reading the Bible, but he also read it to my baby brother. Looking back on things, his apology was part of his peace process.

The night of the funeral, my mother left and went back to the streets. The mourning babies had no mother to wipe their tears. I was surprised and troubled by her leaving. I thought my mother would stay with us at my grandmother's home. I had hoped she would give us the mother we had missed dearly. I hoped she would have shown us more love now that he was out of the picture. Instead of staying and mourning with our family, my mother went to the crack house. The white rocks dried her tears that night. The puff of crack entering her lungs comforted her. That night, we lost her to the black hole she had been trying to escape. The crack dealer and the other crack heads became her family. The streets became her home.

After the funeral, I returned to San Diego broken. I had no clue what my family's future would look like. I had no clue whether my mother would ever overcome her addiction to crack cocaine. I just didn't know. I tried to keep my fears under control, but at times it was unbearable. Now, instead of praying and wishing against the numbness, I welcomed it.

Whenever the numbness lifted, I visited my siblings and grandparents. Seeing their smiles and hearing their voices helped pull me out of depression for a few days. I had grown dependent on those visits. It was as if being in my grandparent's house was a hospital. I went in hanging on for dear life and left feeling revived and ready to tackle life head-on.

During this period, I didn't see my mother much. I only saw her when I was desperate and in need. Whenever I needed rent money, I would drive to find her. I would go to my grandparent's house and pick Jacob up. For some reason, he always knew where she was. He would direct me to drive from crack house to crack house until we found her. I hated it, but I did it because I needed help. One time in particular, my mother got in my back seat. I looked back at her and struggled to not scream or allow the tears to fall. She looked like a skeleton. She had her gold chains draped from her neck. She had rings on her fingers. She had her many earrings in place. Her makeup had been neatly applied. But she looked like death. My heart broke. I couldn't believe she had wasted away. I couldn't believe she was my mother. After getting the $300 I needed for rent, I vowed to never go back. I couldn't take seeing her glassy eyes. I couldn't take hearing her slurred, rapid speech. I couldn't take the smell of crack oozing from her body. I couldn't take the look of death on her face. I just couldn't take it.

That year, I continued to battle kidney infections. Not only was I puzzled, but the doctor was puzzled, as well. No matter how I watched what I ate and drank, they came. I missed more school. My grades had fallen drastically. I constantly felt horrible. I was emotionally numb. I was physically in pain. I was mentally trapped.

To make matters worse, my roommate and I started having problems. Though she and I were close friends, there were times when we didn't speak. I would come home and greet her, only to receive silence in return. I was puzzled because she and I were rarely at home together. The only time we saw each other had been at work. For whatever reason, she treated Nikki and I like crap. Looking back, I think she may have been bipolar or depressed. She had cycles where she'd be sweet as pie, and then become mean and nasty. It became so bad that she even lashed out at us in public.

Living with her became unbearable. I would come home to petty notes written on the bathroom mirror. She would slam doors for no reason, at all times of the night. Whenever she came down from her manic cycles, she would apologize. I would forgive her only for the cycle to restart.

During one of the times we were on good terms, the unthinkable happened. One night after coming home from work, I went straight to sleep. I was extremely tired and my body was in pain. For some reason, I slept peacefully. I didn't feel pain or worry; I just slept. Suddenly, the peace I felt turned into fear. I could feel someone in my room. I just knew it wasn't my roommate. The spirit I felt was unfamiliar and angry. I immediately sat up in my bed.

As I looked towards my bedroom door, I saw a male figure. He stepped in the hallway and proceeded to walk towards my roommate's bedroom. I screamed as loud as I could as I ran to shut my bedroom door. Before my door closed, he turned and ran towards our stairs. After waiting a few minutes, I opened my bedroom door and looked out to see if he was waiting on the stairs. He wasn't. I ran to my roommate's bedroom and woke her up. As I told her what occurred, she grew fearful. We were both extremely scared. Someone had come into our home uninvited. We didn't know who he was or how he had gotten in.

We called the police and waited upstairs for them to come. Once the police arrived, they checked to see if anyone was downstairs. Once it was apparent the area was clear, they called for us to join them downstairs. We were relieved to hear their voices. They told us our front sliding glass door had been unlocked. They asked us whether we had locked it. We both told them we had; we never left our doors unlocked. We both were extremely careful. After taking our statements, we walked to their car and drove around with them.

As we drove, they received a call from another unit. They caught a guy who fit the description we had given. We drove to the location with them. Once there, they told us they would shine the light on the person; all we had to do was identify the intruder. As we peered at the man from the backseat of the police car, I was disappointed. The person I saw wasn't him. As they drove us back to our townhouse, I felt violated and unsafe. He could strike again without warning.

Several nights later, the intruder returned. This night, he didn't enter through the front door as he had done previously. Rather, he entered through my roommate's sliding glass door. He didn't have to pry the door open or pick the lock this time—she had left it cracked to allow air in her bedroom.

Once inside of her bedroom, the intruder lifted her blanket. Unlike most nights, my roommate slept lightly and felt when he lifted her blanket. Instantly, she jumped up out of her bed and started swinging her arms at him. Her boldness caught the intruder by surprise. Instead of fighting her back, he ran out of the sliding glass door down the walkway. My roommate followed behind, hitting him with all her strength. She hit him until he outran her.

Once he reached the gate at the end of the balcony way, he ran down several flights of stairs. At the bottom of the stairs, he jumped into a caramel-colored car and drove off as fast as he could. My roommate was unable to read the license plate because it had been too dark out and she didn't have on her glasses. Again, we called the police. They came out and took a report, encouraging us to keep all doors locked at night.

After that night, I became paranoid. I was scared to death. I watched my back everywhere I went. I was startled by the sound of the slightest noise. I started sleeping with my door closed and locked again. We felt like prisoners in our own home.

Several weeks later, we got a call from the police. The intruder had been caught. The police notified us that the intruder was one of our neighbors. According to the police, he was a serial rapist. They found pictures of women he had taken without their knowledge while they were walking around in our complex inside of his apartment. What was more disturbing was that the police had tied the intruder to other rapes in the complex. He had only been caught because he had tried to rape someone else in the complex. I was relieved. I thought life could go back to normal.

After the intruder incident, things didn't go back to normal—things got worse. My roommate became more disrespectful as the days went on. I hated being at home. I complained to my older sister about everything, which concerned her. I didn't feel comfortable living there and neither did she. She started to constantly worry about me, so she offered me the opportunity to move in with her and her boyfriend. I couldn't resist it; I adored them both. I needed a fresh started. I put in my 30-days' notice and prepared to move.

CHAPTER 10: THE PARENTS WHO GAVE ME A SECOND CHANCE

Moving in with my sister Kamra and her boyfriend Sam was the best thing that could have happened to me. It was with them that I was able to heal; it was with them that I was able to learn myself; it was with them that I was able to be myself.

Shortly after moving in with them, I received the shock of my life. I was academically dismissed from San Diego State University. My grades had fallen below a 2.0 during the time I had been battling kidney infections. Even though I was given two semesters to raise my GPA, I wasn't able to. Each semester, my grades remained low no matter how hard I tried to bring them up. Battling frequent kidney infections coupled with missing a lot of classes and having family issues helped me dig myself into a hole. Everything seemed unreal to me. How would I get out of this? What was I going to do without school? Throughout my entire life, school had been my coping skill. School had never been the problem. Instead of flunking in school, I always managed to do well, if not exceptionally well, despite what I had been going through. I needed school. I couldn't reach my highest goal of becoming an attorney without graduating from school. I couldn't understand how I let this happen.

In that moment, I hated myself. I hated my kidneys for turning on me. I absolutely hated what I had become as a result of the infections. I felt like a complete failure. I had always performed well under adversity until this point. Even though I felt horrible, I immediately researched my options. It was as if the hate fueled me to persevere—I could not throw in the towel. I became desperate for options.

I contacted my school's administration office. As the phone rang, my stomach rose to my throat. I swallowed hard. I was nervous and didn't know what I would say. I hoped and prayed that there would be a way I could get back into school. As I continued to torture myself with my thoughts, I heard a voice on the other end of the phone. The woman recited the customized greeting. After she paused, I blurted out the what, when, where, and how as fast as I could. I was afraid I would miss something, so I didn't even take a breath. After listening without interruption, the woman informed me of my options. I could submit a medical appeal for reinstatement.

I could see the light at the end of the tunnel again. All I had to do was get the doctor to write a letter, write my own letter stating what occurred, and what I planned to do to raise my grades. I felt relieved. I knew the doctor would write the letter on my behalf, and I knew what I needed to do to bring my grades back up.

I hung up the phone inspired and determined. I immediately gathered all of the needed documents with ease. The doctor who had treated me was more than willing to write a letter for me. It even seemed as if he had been more determined then I had been to get me back in school. With the support of my doctor, I worked diligently to get everything taken care of. I did everything in secret, not wanting to tell anyone—not even Nikki. I was embarrassed and ashamed.

Those closest to me never knew the severity or the frequency of my kidney infections. I hid the pain I was experiencing. I had learned from my childhood the art of suffering in silence. My motto became, "no one needs to know unless they can do something to help." As far as I was concerned, nothing but antibiotics and pain medication could help me. So, there was no reason to talk about my feelings. My feelings were mine and mine alone. Besides, the one person I had opened up to was no longer there. I felt no need to open up to anyone anymore.

After submitting the medical appeal, I waited anxiously for the verdict. I prayed and asked God to work everything out. I needed school to survive. I had no backup plan. I had planned my life out. I knew from the age of four that I would go to college and then to law school. I needed to graduate from college to make a difference.

As I waited for the verdict, life seemed to be moving in slow motion. My thoughts were consumed with "what ifs." As I waited, I felt like I was going to die of anxiety. Shortly after submitting my appeal, I received a decision letter. As I opened the letter, I held my breath. I wanted to look, but I also didn't want to. This single decision had the potential to keep me on course or stir me off course. I hadn't decided how I would respond to the decision. I hadn't thought past getting the letter.

I read it quickly as I held my breath and prayed for mercy. I read it as if the words would escape the page right before my eyes. I was relieved. My future as an attorney was real again. I had been reinstated back into school. The best part about it all was that I didn't have to miss a semester. After receiving the good news, I was able to enjoy the remainder of my summer break from school.

That fall, I was required to repeat the courses I had done poorly in. Instead of being upset, I viewed it as an opportunity to get things correct, once and for all. I knew it was mandatory that I got my act together. I knew missing assignments or class was not an option. I decided I would sit in the front row of every class. I also decided I would sit in class whether or not my body was riddled with pain.

The period that I experienced being academically dismissed and reinstated in school was the start to a new season of my life. I learned to laugh without inhibition. I learned to live in the moment. Living with Kamra and Sam taught me so much. There were many days and nights that I listened to their loud laughter as I sat in my bedroom alone. I sat there alone not because I wasn't welcomed to join them, but because I didn't know how.

My sister would periodically knock on my bedroom door to check on me. Each time, she stuck her head inside to ask if I was okay. The small voice inside of me screamed, "No, I'm not! Please help me to be carefree like you guys."

To them I was weird, and to me, they were weird. They were accustomed to laughing, interacting with each other, and enjoying life. I had grown accustom to being alone, laughing on the inside, and working to survive.

A part of me adored them for being so free. They were free to express their feelings. They were free to be who they were. I wanted to be like them, but didn't know how. I truly didn't know what it was like to be free. I had been bound for so long. So, I continued to sit in my bedroom afraid, secretly wanting to join them. I just didn't know how to behave around them.

The more I declined her offers, the more it seemed like my sister would ask. If was as if she was on a quest to make me feel welcomed. It seemed as though she wouldn't stop asking until I gave in. They wanted to include me in everything. It felt weird at first. I felt extremely self-conscious. I worried about saying the wrong thing or acting awkwardly. I drove myself completely crazy with the thoughts until I finally gave in. I faced my fear and just let go.

After being around them for a while, I felt myself laughing without shame. Over time, I learned to be free. I learned to allow my suppressed inner child run wild and free. I loved the freedom I had found with my sister and Sam.

I was able to be free from negative feelings towards men. There, I was living in an apartment with a male who never crept in my bedroom at night. There, I learned that there was such a thing as being close with and loving a male without feeling uncomfortable. Sam had become like a brother to me. Sam was my protector. Sam taught me a lot about men and proper dating. I was able to confide in him about almost everything.

Sam would look out for me whenever my friends and I would go out with him. He always made sure we were safe. He always made sure we all returned to our cars and home safely. It was as if we had our own personal body guard. Sam was like the father I never had. He was much more than a brother. He was the first man, aside from my brothers, who never betrayed me.

Not only had Sam never betrayed me, but Kamra didn't either. She was always there for me. I always felt as though I could tell her the crazy truth about guys I had dated without being judged. Often times, she would burst out laughing as she said in a high pitched tone, "Roszien, I can't believe you. You're crazy." I lived for those moments. I was exploring who I was in many ways. In those very moments, I was allowed to let my walls down. I knew she wouldn't judge me. I knew she would tell me the truth. If I was wrong about something, she would say it. If she didn't agree with something, she would say it. I knew without a doubt I could trust her with my life.

Life with them gave me courage to go on. The first semester I went back to school after being academically dismissed was difficult. I constantly worried about being kicked out of school for good. I was in complete fear every single day. To make things more difficult, my kidneys continued to get infected. It seemed as if no matter how much I took care of myself, the infections still came. I was scared, yet courageous. Living with them gave me the courage I needed to step out and press through the pain. With them I learned to laugh even if I was uncomfortable doing it. I learned to penetrate the surface and dig deep within myself. I learned to pull out strength instead of pity, because I had been set free.

I managed to get through that first semester back. There were many times when I had to sit in class holding my back as I took notes and took exams. I raised my hands and answered questions through the pain. I did the opposite from what I had done the previous semesters. It was all because I had learned to live a different way. I learned to allow the little girl inside to run free. I had learned to allow her to continue to dream. I had learned to do the unthinkable.

At the end of my second semester post reinstatement, my GPA rose above a 2.0. I had managed to turn things around! Even though my class load was heftier than before, I excelled. I became more focused and more determined to achieve my goals. With a support system, I was well on my way. For the first time in college, and in many years, my dreams had started to become my reality. I was happy internally *and* externally. I was doing well in school. I had people who loved, supported, and believed in me. I felt as though the only way to go from there was up. My past was a distant memory. I was over everything that had occurred to me as a child. Or so I thought.

CHAPTER 11: AND HERE COMES PTSD

After living with Kamra and Sam for a little shy of two years, I decided it was time to spread my wings. Like a protective parent, Kamra didn't think it was time. She tried to talk me out of it. She couldn't understand why I suddenly had a desire to move. She asked question after question. She even tried to convince me it would be too hard for me. I could have taken offense, but I didn't. Kamra had every right to be worried.

I was only 21 years old at the time. I had never lived on my own. But my mind was made up. I wanted to experience living completely alone. I loved living with Kamra and Sam so much. I was comfortable. In fact, I had never been that comfortable in my life. I had never felt *that* secure. I knew if I didn't leave, I would never want to leave. So I mustered up my strength and courage to go apartment hunting. After a brief time, I found an apartment seven minutes away from them.

Living alone was one of the most liberating experiences. I felt like I was *actually* an adult. I was responsible for all of the bills. I could have company over whenever I wanted. I could also refuse to have company whenever I wanted. I was in complete control.

Shortly after living on my own, I met Jade while out partying with my friends. Jade was tall, kind, and handsome. We enjoyed each other's company. We would spend hours with each other in the evenings and on weekends. The thought of being separated from him became unbearable. I wanted him near me as much as possible. My feelings for him grew more and more with each passing day until I was in love with him.

As things progressed along well, we decided it was best to make some changes. We decided to live together. Instead of getting another place, we decided Jade would move in with me. We were both thrilled. I felt like nothing could possibly go wrong. I was in love! I could see wedding bells in our future! I felt like I was living a life full of love and endless happiness.

Unfortunately, my happy bubble was popped. As I sat on my living room couch watching television while Jade was away, the unthinkable happened. Images from the nights I had been molested flooded my mind. For the first time in my life, I felt the pain, horror, trauma, and hopelessness I should have felt years ago. I felt as though the molestation had just happened. I instantly became afraid and sick to my stomach. There was no sign of the numbness I had felt as a child. I couldn't stop the images. I felt every ounce of pain. I suddenly started to cry out of nowhere as my body curled into a tight ball. I cried hard for what seemed like an eternity until the images stopped playing.

I had many more episodes after the first one. I was both confused and concerned. The monster was dead. There was no possible way it could happen again. I couldn't understand why I had started to experience the flashbacks. Was I crazy? What if the images surfaced when I was home with Jade? What if the images flooded my mind while I was in public? Why was it happening? I just didn't understand. I knew I couldn't be trapped in this type of fear. I did the only thing I knew how to do—I enrolled myself into therapy.

Therapy was one of the most unforgettable experiences I've ever had with a stranger. Each therapy session made me feel as though I really mattered. The focus of each session was on my childhood trauma. I was allowed to pour out all of my emotions, thoughts, and feelings every week in a safe environment. I didn't, for the first time, worry about how I looked. I wasn't concerned about being judged; I was only concerned about healing. I wanted the intrusive flashbacks to stop once and for all. I wanted to fearlessly face the tragedies of my past.

Therapy was the first time anyone had asked me about my feelings. Initially, I was completely uncomfortable. I couldn't even describe how I felt. I had to really dig deep to find my feelings. Once I found the words to describe my true feelings, they came out fast. For the first time, I heard myself say I felt violated, abandoned, helpless, hopeless, mistaken, like a trouble maker, disgusting, numb, and hurt, as well as other things. It felt really good getting my emotions all out. It felt as if the little girl inside was being freed more and more with each session.

By the end of my therapy season, I felt whole. I cried until I had no tears left. The flashbacks went away. I came to understand that I did nothing wrong. I understood what happened to me was not my fault. Talking about everything released me. I was finally free from the monsters at night.

With each therapy session, things at home changed. For whatever reason, Jade and I started to fall out of love. Things became weird between us. We loved each other, but we weren't really *in love* with each other. Jade revealed to me that he hadn't been where he wanted to be in life. I guess he started to feel as if he wasn't good watching me strive towards what I wanted to be. We were definitely going in different directions. We ultimately decided to end our relationship.

Although the relationship was over, we continued to live together. Our lease hadn't ended yet. Jade didn't want to leave me bearing all the bills, and he wasn't ready to move, either. He still needed to work his living situation out. Even though continuing to live together seemed like it was for the best, it wasn't. It was very challenging at first. As time passed, it got easier.

Living with Jade beyond the failed relationship was a teacher. We learned to respect each other's boundaries even more. We learned to sleep in the same bed without touching each other. We learned the art of communicating beyond emptiness and pain. What started as a difficult experience turned into a great and unexpected lesson.

CHAPTER 12: THE LETTER THAT CHANGED MY LIFE

After graduating from college, I decide to take a year off before applying to law school. I needed that time to decompress. I needed that time to enjoy life before the biggest phase of my life started. I had overcome all the obstacles placed in my life by graduating with a BA in Psychology and a BS in Criminal Justice Administration. I deserved the break.

During my year off, I applied to as many law schools as possible. I was determined that I would stay in California. I had absolutely no desire to move out of the state. My mind was set; I would get accepted into my school of choice. I wasn't moving out of California. Unfortunately, this didn't happen.

My LSAT score wasn't great and I had an average GPA . I received rejection letter after rejection letter from different law schools. For the second time in my life, my dream of going to law school looked impossible. I became worried and anxious as the days went by. All I could think was, "what will I do if I don't get into law school?" My biggest fear now seemed to be my reality.

After facing my reality, I devised a backup plan. I applied to work as a probation officer. By then, I had almost lost all hope of going to law school. Being an attorney seemed out of my reach. I had given up hope until I had a life-changing conversation with one of my dearest friends Christina.

Christina had the perfect solution to my problem. She suggested I apply to Thomas M. Cooley law school. Christina made this suggestion because she knew it had been my heart's desire to go to law school. She also knew I would listen to her because I always followed her advice. That evening Christina gave me the strength I needed to believe in my dream of going to law school. I regained hope. I started to believe being an attorney was possible again.

Though I wasn't fond of moving out of state, I applied to law school in Michigan. I was nervous, yet comforted by the fact that Christina had been living in Michigan for a few years. She had already known the area, and if she survived, I knew I would too.

As I submitted my application, I prayed. Prior to that day, I never put any decision in God's hand. I did what I wanted without consulting God. But that day, I told God I would go wherever He wanted me to go.

As I waited for an answer from Thomas M. Cooley, I received the last two responses I had been waiting for from California law schools. Both letters invited me to attend their summer programs. Each school promised to admit me into the fall 2008 class if I performed well. These letters gave me hope. I knew if Cooley didn't accept me I had somewhere to go. I knew my dream would be possible. I still continued to wait on the acceptance letter from Cooley before accepting a conditional admittance to a California school.

As I awaited the final letter, a response from my application to be a probation officer arrived. My application was accepted. I was given a test date to take the required exam. I was happy, but not excited. Being a probation officer was plan B, not plan A. I now refused to give up on my dream and accept plan B. So, I continued to wait and pray.

One day prior to going to work, I checked the mail. I had a feeling something important was in the mail for me. At that time, I usually waited until after work to check the mail. But that day, I broke my routine and checked it early. When I opened the mailbox, I saw a large envelope inside. I knew it had to be the acceptance letter I was waiting for because I had received all the other letters from the other law schools.

As I opened the letter, I was relieved. My assumptions were true. I was going to law school! God had answered my prayer! I didn't care that I had to move outside of California. I didn't care that I would be starting over. All I cared about was making my dream a reality.

The remainder of that summer, I prepared to relocate to Michigan. I sent my letter of acceptance to Cooley and applied for financial aid. I located an apartment and sent in the deposit as required. I got rid of all of my furniture and the belongings I would not take with me. I saved as much money as possible for the journey. I decided to take my younger sister along with me.

CHAPTER 13: MICHIGAN, HERE WE COME

My mother, my sister Donnika, and I piled into my Mazda 3 and drove from Los Angeles, California to Lansing, Michigan. Throughout the drive, Donnika cried almost the entire time. She experienced mixed emotions. She had just graduated from high school and she had never been away from family let alone outside of California. To say she was scared was an understatement, but she was crazy enough to listen to my mother and I. I had this great plan to help her during her first two years of college. At that time, it seemed like the ultimate plan that would lead her down a road to success. I was thrilled she had decided to come with me. I was certain she and I would grow closer than we had ever been before. After being in the car for close to 2 days without stopping to rest, we made it to Lansing safely.

As we drove down the streets of downtown Lansing, I had many thoughts. Lansing was completely different from what I expected. "Wow," I thought as my eyes searched the scene. Lansing was definitely different from both Los Angeles and San Diego. I experienced instant culture shock. The people looked differently, dressed differently, and acted differently. My sister and I would definitely stick out like a sore thumb. My sister felt the same way. I remember her sitting in the backseat crying even harder than she had on the drive to Lansing. I instantly questioned myself. What had we signed up for? What had I gotten myself into? Whatever it was, I knew there was no turning back. I had given up everything to follow my dreams. I had nothing to turn back to. For the time being, this was my life and I was determined to make the most of it.

After we arrived in Lansing, my mother stayed with us for a couple of days before returning to California. While she was with us, she helped us settle in as much as possible. We bought a few things for our empty apartment. We couldn't afford furniture at that time. I didn't have a lot of resources to purchase much. I had funded the entire trip, paid the deposit, and paid the first month's rent for the apartment. All I could afford to buy was food, an air mattress, a black futon, a TV stand, and a TV from a secondhand store. I was accustomed to a fully furnished apartment. I was a little heartbroken that I couldn't afford more, but I knew this was my portion for the time being. Instead of complaining, I remained positive. I had faith things wouldn't always be the way they were.

The first change we experienced was saying goodbye to our mother. We had both grown used to living without her, but this was different. We would now be living 2,200 miles away from her. We wouldn't be able to jump in a car or on a short bus ride to her when we had emergencies. She wouldn't be able to come to us, either. The goodbye was bittersweet. This goodbye was necessary. My sister and I mustered up all the strength we had and said goodbye. That day, we left the airport without knowing when we would see her again.

Driving away from the airport that day felt surreal. Had we really driven over 2,200 miles just for me to go to law school? Had I really convinced my sister to come along the crazy ride with me? Was I really responsible for her? Was I really starting law school? These were just a few of the questions that ran through my mind that day. It wasn't until several weeks later that everything hit me. I really gave up everything I had and dragged my sister along to fulfill my dream of going to law school. That night, we sat on our living room floor talking about what we had done. We suddenly burst out in tears. We looked around our empty apartment and cried even harder. We had little money. We had no family nearby. We couldn't believe what we had done. We had in fact left the comfort we had for the unknown.

My sorrow turned into joy once classes started. During orientation and the first week of class, I managed to find people who liked doing the same things I enjoyed. Prior to going to law school, I promised myself I would be totally focused and wouldn't party. I was under the impression that everyone in law school would be focused on getting high grades, getting on law review, and getting a great job as well. But that was not the case. Many law students were focused on creating lasting memories and friendships, too. I quickly learned to assimilate. My crew and I went to class, studied Monday through Thursday, and partied nearly every Thursday through Sunday.

That term, I spent less time at home than I previously expected. I went to class, then to work, then to the library to study until it closed. When I got home, I would stay up past 3 a.m. studying before going to bed. I would sleep for a couple of hours before getting back up and doing it all over again.

During this time, I hardly spent any time with my sister. There were occasions when we would randomly jump in the car to go shopping, and on many nights, I would return from studying with a huge appetite we would go to Denny's. Aside from the random outings, we spent very little together.

I was too busy enjoying my life to even recognize the signs that Donnika was depressed. Sure, I would come home to find her sleeping or closed up in her dark room, but I didn't think anything of it because it usually was late in the evening. I didn't pay attention to the occasions where I caught her crying. I assumed Donnika was still grieving over the death of her boyfriend. Or maybe it was my selfishness that kept me from even asking what was wrong.

I was naïve. I thought and envisioned everything would go well for my sister. I thought she would go to school, meet great friends, and find herself. I never considered the possibility that things would go differently. I wasn't even prepared for the outcome of anything going any other way than I had planned. I still saw her as my little sister. When I looked at her I saw a smiling little girl, not a young woman trying to find herself in a big world of possibilities. I had been too concerned with what I wanted for her to ask her what she wanted for herself.

Despite her depression, Donnika kept her grades up. She had managed to not allow her sadness affect her to the point where she would do poorly in school. During that time, she rarely missed school. She got an A in almost all of her classes. I was proud of her, and I thought my plans for her life had worked perfectly.

As Donnika's second semester started, I was slapped in the face with the reality that she had another plan for her life. Unlike her first semester, Donnika met new people. Initially I was excited for her; I no longer had to feel guilty about leaving her alone. She had such a life of her own that I would come home to an empty apartment. I could no longer randomly pop in and ask her to accompany me to the store or the mall. She had a life of her own that did not involve me. She was finally spreading her wings.

While she spread her wings, I was introduced to the man I planned on marrying and having children with. One evening, my sister invited me to attend her friend's birthday dinner. Initially I declined because I felt too old to go. However, after being asked over and over again, I decided to go. I loved food. I had nothing else planned. It wouldn't hurt. I was up for a few laughs, so I went. Little did I know I would meet Maurice. I didn't expect to connect with him, but I did, and it was all because of one invite. I never imagined my sister's new-found freedom would result in me meeting anyone, let alone the man I would fall madly in love with.

Donnika's new-found freedom was welcomed until her grades started to fall. My sister was spending so much time having fun that she neglected her studies. It was during this time that I became nagging and overbearing. I couldn't just allow her to go down the road I went down. I couldn't just allow her to ruin the plans I had for her life. In my mind, I still knew what was best for her. I was determined that she was going to do as I said, even if it meant forcing her. I had the illusion that she would straighten up. I had the illusion that she was going to listen to everything I told her. I would call and question her about homework and her whereabouts. Instead of telling me the truth, she lied. Once I discovered her lies, we would argue to the point of almost fighting. She was standing her ground and I was upset because "my little sister" wasn't listening to me. I didn't like the little feisty, independent woman she had become; she was now messing up my plans for her.

The harder I pushed, the worse things became. Donnika was convinced she knew what was best for her life while I had been convinced I knew what was best for the both of our lives. My sister and I started to drift apart. The arguments grew more heated. I became concerned for her. I didn't want to be responsible for her decisions. I didn't want my family to blame me if anything happened to her. So, I decided I would send her home when the semester ended.

Donnika was not happy about the decision. I didn't ask her for her opinion. When I told her she was going home, she asked me to give her another chance. She promised she would do better. She promised to raise her grades. I didn't listen. My mind had already been made up. I couldn't deal with the thought of something happening to her. I faced the the fact that she was grown and would be making her own choice regardless of what I had to say. No matter how much she pleaded with me to give her another chance, I stood my ground and sent her home.

My sister leaving was bittersweet for me. Even though I knew it was the best decision, it tore me up inside. I really thought we would become closer but instead we were torn apart. My sister felt like I was sending her away because I wanted her out of the picture to spend more time with Maurice. But that wasn't the case. I loved my baby sister but didn't know how to deal with her being all grown up. I couldn't deal with the possibility that she was free to decide for herself. I couldn't let her see me break down. I was an emotional wreck inside, but I masked it with a smile.

CHAPTER 14: IN THE BEGINNING

When I met Maurice, I wasn't romantically interested in him, but I fell in love with him quickly. He was well-spoken and polite. The day we met, I invited him to join my friends and I later that evening. He actually laughed and questioned my age. I was flattered. I'm not sure if it had been his nonchalant attitude or the fact that he wasn't paying any attention to me that sparked my interest, but whatever it was, I was interested. I had to know him.

That night, I told my sister to pass my number along. I had to be certain we would connect. As I got dressed that night for the club, I hoped I would see him. I was intrigued and I didn't know why. There was something about him that really sparked my interest. Maybe it was his smile. Maybe it has been his brown skin. Whatever it was, I was interested.

When I arrived at the club that night, I looked over the crowed for Maurice. I had hoped he would come, but he didn't show up. I was disappointed. Several long days later, Maurice finally called. By that time, I had given up on the idea of him calling. I had learned over the years that if a guy didn't call within the first couple of days, they weren't going to call. But to my surprise, he called. I felt the butterflies in my stomach as we spoke. This feeling was new to me again. Speaking to an attractive man was all too common to me because I had dated so much, but I felt flutters during every conversation with Maurice.

After a few phone conversations, Maurice invited me to the gym with him. Even though I was used to getting invitations by guys, I was surprised that our first interaction involved the gym. I wasn't sure if it had been a mid-west thing or what. The majority of the guys I dated invited me to dinner, the movies, dessert tasting, or to a lounge. Instead of being difficult, I accepted the invitation.

The day we went to the gym, I picked him up. I was a little nervous. I didn't know what to expect. When he got in the car, I questioned everything. As I glanced at him, I even questioned whether I was attracted to him. The guys I dated were very clean-cut; Maurice was the opposite. He had neat little twists and wore basketball attire. He didn't speak properly like the other guys. In fact, I had to learn the meaning of certain words to keep up. Nevertheless, I swallowed my uncertainties and drove to the gym.

As soon as we arrived to the gym, my nervousness grew to an all-time high. Not only were we not the only ones there, but I was also the only woman there. I wanted to run out and sit in the car until he was done, or just go home. My heart was beating extremely fast at this point. I felt like I had a target on my back. I kept asking myself why had I come. I was uncomfortable. I was completely out of my element. I didn't know what to do, so I sat down right where I stood and watched the game.

With each passing moment, the tension I felt in my body started to ease. I found myself enjoying the game. I like basketball, so it wasn't too hard for me to become entertained. Finally, after playing a few games, Maurice came over to me. He motioned for me to follow him. We went to a smaller court located through a separate door. He threw a basketball to me. I caught it and shot. He was surprised. He started to tease me by saying I didn't know what I was doing. I flashed him a smile and we started to play one-on-one. I really didn't know what I was doing, but I kept up. Our bodies were too close a few times. Instead of moving away, I stayed right there. I was nervous yet fascinated by the close contact. It was something I had never experienced. I was on a mission to stay in that moment as long as possible.

That night was the start of something intense. We saw each other as often as we could. We would watch TV, go out to eat, and talk for hours. We were forming a real friendship. Even though we had been attracted to each other, we kept things as innocent as possible. I can't tell you exactly when things started to shift between us, but when it turned, it turned quickly. He started to call and text me more often than usual. I was flattered. He even went as far as offering to bring me coffee to the library during my nightly study sessions. He would even wait for me to finish studying after 1 a.m. just to come over and spend time with me. At that time, he seemed perfect. I was falling hard for him.

Forming strong feelings for Maurice presented a problem. I already had an attachment with someone. Although I dated guys, there was one in particular that I really liked. Rob and I had met in the library one evening during my first few weeks of law school. He was extremely handsome, polite, had a great personality, nice teeth, a beautiful smile, clean-cut, and intelligent. We connected one evening after making eye contact. Prior to that night, I watched him as he studied. I wanted to get to know him. I looked forward to seeing him at the library. I would get disappointed when I didn't see him.

After a short conversation between study sessions, he and I started talking. We even developed a routine of meeting on the same floor at the same table of the library. Our innocent looks over our computers, books, and outlines quickly turned into flirtation. When it became apparent that we both had a strong interest in each other, we started spending time together outside of the library. We talked about everything. We enjoyed each other's company. There had never been any complications. There hadn't been any drama. I never worried about his attention being on anyone or anything else. He never even looked at his phone when we were together.

Things between Rob and I continued to go well until he revealed to me that he never wanted any children. I wanted children. The thought of having a serious relationship with a man who didn't want children was out of the question. I continued to enjoy his company after this discovery, but I knew that things couldn't become serious.

We continued to spend time together on a regular basis until he graduated. When he graduated, Rob relocated back to D.C. We tried to keep in contact with each other, but it was hard. It was during this time I met Maurice. I still had feelings for Rob, but I was also interested in Maurice.

After about a month of the madness, I decided to visit Rob in D.C. I told myself prior to going that I would decide who I would cut off. I knew I didn't want to continue down the road I had been on. I knew I was getting to a point where I wanted to settle down, or at least focus more attention on only one man.

During the trip to D.C., I had a wonderful time. It was as if we were back in Michigan and no time had lapsed. I loved being in Rob's presence. There was so much peace and security. There was so much excitement and joy. I missed what we shared with each other. I didn't want to leave at all, but I knew I would have to return to school. I also knew I would have to make a decision. I asked Rob whether he ever wanted to have children in hopes he had changed his mind. I wanted him to change his mind. I wanted to pursue something more serious with him. I was open to the possibility of being in a relationship with him, even if it had to be long distance. I held my breath as I waited for the answer to the single most important question. As I had expected and feared, Rob still didn't want to have children. Instead of accepting a simple "no," I asked follow-up questions. I needed to know why. Maybe I was hoping there would be a way that I could talk him into wanting kids or shed some light on his reasoning. I was desperate.

My desperation for the answer I wanted was stopped dead in its tracks. Rob didn't want children because he felt children were too much responsibility. My hopes of having anything with Rob died that day in D.C. I enjoyed the remainder of the trip with Rob. I stared at him when he wasn't watching a little bit longer than usual. I was soaking every inch of him up because I knew I would never see him again.

Once I returned from D.C., Maurice and I continued to see each other. We spent more time with each other than before. We grew closer together in the process. We became intimate for the first time, too. I never imaged things would progress so quickly. I don't know if it had been because I was trying to get over Rob. Whatever the reason had been, things moved quickly. I stopped talking to the few guys I still entertained. The fear I once had about being in a relationship disappeared as I started to trust Maurice. I purposely allowed my walls that I had built to come crumbling down. I let go of all of the misconceptions that I had about athletes. I simply let go.

As the months went by, I fell in love with Maurice. I loved his smile. I loved his language. I loved his sense of humor. I loved the fact that we came from two different worlds. I loved seeing him with his two daughters. At that moment in time, there had not been anything I didn't love about him. In my mind, he seemed perfect.

My perfect view of him came crushing down six months into our relationship. I had taken a trip to visit my family in California. I was excited to see my grandparents. I still remember the glow my grandfather wore that day. He looked more radiant than I had ever seen him. After sending time with my grandparents, my mother, siblings, and I left. About an hour later, my mother received a phone call. My grandfather unexpectedly passed away. Instead of staying until the funeral, I flew back to school with plans of returning for the funeral. I needed to keep things as normal as possible. I needed to make sure my grades did not slip.

I thought I would be able to be strong until I returned back to my family, but I couldn't. I had a lot of break downs. I was over 2,200 miles away from my family, and hurting. I didn't know how to process everything or deal with the pain. My grandfather was the first person I had been close to who passed away. I assumed Maurice would be there for me. I assumed he would hold me. To my surprise, he wasn't. One day as I sat in my living room, I started to cry uncontrollably. In that moment, I needed him to hold me. A soft touch or a warm hug was all I wanted. I hadn't ever felt that type of pain before in my life. I needed comfort. Instead of offering me comfort, Maurice got up and left me alone.

At the time, I couldn't understand why Maurice had abandoned me when I needed him the most. I thought that maybe him seeing me so emotional was too difficult for him, or that maybe he didn't know how to approach me at that moment. I forgave him—something I wish I had not done because leaving me alone at the most valuable times became a running theme in our relationship.

Maurice's past, or what I had assumed was in his past, started to interfere with our relationship. One day, his youngest daughter's mother started to attack my character unprovoked. Aside from seeing her at a basketball game or two, I had never spoken to her before in my life. I had no desire to see her or talk about her. As far as I was concerned, she had been the past and I didn't have any reason to interact with her. Our relationship was still new, so there was no need for a formal meeting. At that time, I was not trying to marrying him nor was I trying to play step-mom to her daughter. I was simply trying to figure things out with Maurice.

I had no desire to entertain his past when I was focusing on building our present. But with the constant slandering of my reputation and name on social media, I had to face the music. Maurice's baby's mother went as far as telling his family I had been cheating on him. To my surprise, his family believed her. I found myself constantly defending my every move. If she saw me at a bar or a club, she picked up the phone and called everyone she could with bizarre stories. Maurice knew she was lying, yet he still entertained the drama by questioning me about her claims. I was baffled. I couldn't understand why someone would go out of their way to assassinate my character.

Defending my reputation had become an almost daily occurrence. I started to become stressed and worried about my future with Maurice. I felt alone. I was angry and couldn't understand why I had been targeted. I couldn't understand why Maurice's past had become relevant in our relationship. I didn't realize the past had actually been the present. I had been naive and gullible. I believed every word Maurice told me. I asked him whether I had a reason to be worried, and Maurice always replied "no." I had no other reason to doubt him, so I ignored the rumors.

The more I remained calm and ignored the rumors, the more things started to escalate. One day as I was driving down the street, someone appeared to be following me. At first, I thought I was driving too slow, so I changed lanes. The person also changed lanes behind me. I changed lanes again to be sure that I was being followed. Sure enough, the person changed lanes too. After looking through my rearview mirror, I noticed it was Maurice's ex. I was pissed. As I drove slower, she drove slower. When I sped up, she sped up. I became more upset. Instead of calling anyone, I turned my music up as loud as it could go. That day, I had been listening to gansta rap, feeling empowered. I didn't care what would end up happening as long as she got the message that I wasn't running from her. I was prepared to fight if I had to. At that moment, every lie she told came to mind. I was ready to smash her face. I hoped she would do something stupid so that I could claim self-defense for what I was going to do. Thankfully for her, she stopped following me as soon as I turned left.

A few weeks after I was followed, there was an incident at a club. That night, I had gone out with Maurice, his cousins, and other individuals. We were celebrating his brother girlfriend's 40th birthday. As we danced, I started to feel as though something strange would occur. My feelings were confirmed when Maurice abruptly stopped dancing and led me back to VIP. Later that night as we stood on the second floor, one of his ex's friends walked up to me. She had been talking on the phone with someone. I heard her say, "they right here in front of me." I instantly knew his daughter's mother was on the phone. I responded, "you don't know me and don't have anything to do with this." The friend continued to talk and laugh. Maurice pulled me by the arm. I was upset. I called the friend out of her name and told Maurice I was tired of everything. We walked back into VIP. The friend followed behind and started to make a scene. In that moment anger took over and I was ready to smash her face in. Unfortunately, no one would allow her to get close to me. After a few moments of drama, everyone cleared VIP. I sat there enraged. I had never been disrespected like that before. Maurice sat next to me. I took my earrings off and told him "it's whatever." In that moment, I had prepared myself for the unknown battle I would walk into. I knew that if I didn't face what was on the other side of the door, things wouldn't get any easier. I knew I had to stand up for myself once and for all.

I walked to my car where Maurice's family had been waiting. There had been other issues in the parking lot that night, so police cars were present in the far end. After getting in the car, I put on my seat belt. Seconds later, I heard a knock on my window. I looked up and saw a heavy-set, light-skinned female wearing all black. I took my seat belt off. Maurice told me to stay in the car as he got out, but I didn't listen. I opened the door. By this time, the woman had walked back to her driver's side door yelling threats. I was yelling, "y'all not going to scare me!" I was ready to go blow to blow. At that moment, I wasn't thinking about school. I wasn't thinking about the consequences. I just knew I needed to protect myself. With every rumor, I kept my mouth closed. When I was followed, I didn't do anything. I was tired of the nonsense. I was determined to set things straight once and for all.

Before I could make my way to the unknown woman's car door, the police were surrounding us. A female officer asked me to get back in the car. I politely explained the situation to her. Afterwards, I agreed to get in the car and leave if they would take care of the situation. The officer told her to get in her car, as well. She continued to argue and shout threats. Maurice's mother and cousin were out of my car by this time. His mother walked towards the back of the female's car to obtain her license plate number. It was during this time that his mother saw Maurice's baby's mother hiding in the car's back seat. She, too, wore all black. After a few moments of madness, I got back in my car. I was done with the drama. It made no sense to argue. I sat in my car waiting for the woman to move from behind me. She continued to argue with Maurice until the officer placed her under arrest. Once another officer removed her car, we were able to leave.

As we drove home that night, the woman's identity was released. She was Maurice's daughter's older cousin. I was beyond annoyed by this point. I couldn't understand why there had been so much drama. I wanted no part of the drama. I, unlike everyone else involved, had too much at risk. That Monday, I filed a restraining order against Maurice's daughter's mother. The restraining order was granted immediately, and I was relieved. She finally stopped writing about me on Facebook, she no longer followed me, and no one else approached me on her behalf.

The restraining order made things worse. After she was unsuccessfully in getting the restraining order removed, she filed a restraining order on me. I couldn't believe her. As I read the statements she made, my mouth dropped. Not only did she allege I followed her but she alleged I showed up to his family events, spread rumors on Facebook about her, and other things. Everything she had done to me she turned it around as if I had done it to her. She even went as far as to state I was upset because she was pregnant by Maurice and I couldn't take it. I immediately questioned Maurice. Deep down I knew there was more to the story. I knew she wasn't acting crazy for no apparent reason. Maurice response was always "I haven't messed with her. She always claim she's pregnant by me when she get mad. That ain't nothing new." His mother even confirmed what Maurice had said. Even though I didn't believe him completely, I left it go. I knew what was done in the dark would come to the light.

The judge granted her ex-parte restraining order against me. I immediately responded and filed for a court date to have the restraining order dropped. I hired my friend who was an attorney to represent me. I knew I had to show her I wasn't playing with her. At the hearing, Maurice's mother and cousin were there to testify. After hearing the testimony, the judge dropped the restraining order. He publicly admonished her for her behavior. That day, I finally felt like someone had protected me

CHAPTER 15: THE KNOCK THAT CHANGE THE COURSE OF MY LIFE

I had no idea God would start to call me as soon as he did. I thought He would save me when I was older. At that time, I was only 26 years old. I loved partying. I loved drinking. I loved fornicating. I loved wearing short dresses. I loved cursing. I loved focusing on myself. I was totally in love with the life style I had been living. I thought I was in the greatest relationship of my life. I was living my dream.

In the midst of my false belief of perfection, God softly knocked. One day out of the blue, I woke up with a great desire to go to church. Instead of giving in, I kept pushing it to the back of my mind. I kept telling myself I would go one day. The more I tried to bury the thought, the louder it became. It started to invade my study sessions. It invaded my down time. It even invaded my dreams. It was as if I was being haunted. I felt as though I had a monkey on my back. No matter how hard I tried to shake it off, I couldn't. After failed attempts to silence the monkey, I gave in. I reached for the phone and called the one person I knew could guide me—I called my friend Christina.

Christina was the only friend I had known who was completely sold out to God. She and I would go to church together during our first year in college. She was the ultimate example of what it looked like to be young and saved. Unlike the rest of us, she didn't give in to temptation. She was kind and loving. She didn't curse or lie. Not only was she still a virgin, but she had never kissed a man. She truly honored the Lord with her body and her life.

When Christina heard that I wanted to go to church with her, she was thrilled. She even offered to pick me up that upcoming Sunday. I asked a lot of questions as if my life depended on this single decision. At the time, I didn't even realize it did. At first, I was skeptical because the pastor was young. I was used to going to church where the pastor was the same age as my grandfather. I falsely assumed that all pastors needed to be dirt old in order to be anointed and saved. Even though I was skeptical, I still decided to accept Christina's invitation to church that upcoming Sunday.

My experience at Epic Center of Worship was insane. I was blown away from the moment I stepped foot in the front door. I had never seen so many young people worshiping God in one place. I had never seen praise dancers who wore paint on their faces. I had never seen flags being incorporated into praise dancing before. I had never felt the spirit of God with such intensity. I sat with a million thoughts and many emotions surging through my body.

Although my initial experience at Epic Center was one of shock, I was still amazed. Deep down, I knew I had found where I needed to be. I knew about God, but had never experienced Him for myself. I knew in order for me to get to know God, I needed Epic Center and everything it had to offer. I knew the power of God I felt would break the chains of bondage I had been under. I knew, without fully understanding, God had led me there.

After that first trip to Epic Center, I kept going. I not only attended Sunday service, but I also started going to Bible study and other programs. The more I went to Epic Center, the more I wanted to know about Jesus. The more I listened to my then Pastor Sean Holland preach illustrated sermons, the more I wanted to know Jesus. The more I desired to know Jesus, the more I thought about Jesus.

My desire for Jesus grew to the point that I arranged my life around church. I no longer picked classes based on their availability; I picked my class schedule based on my ability to attend Wednesday night Bible study. I even refused to take classes that interfered with the

Monday afternoon law student Bible studies. I developed such a hunger for the Word of God that could only be satisfied by hearing it.

I was very fortunate to be taught the unadulterated Word of God by my pastor. He was totally surrendered to God and His word. He had a passion to make disciples out of all of those who were assigned to him. He made many sacrifices to make sure his church had a true understanding of God's word. For example, He had several weekly bible studies to ensure every age group learned the word of God. Pastor Holland never added to or took away from God's word as he taught us, and he urged us to do the same.

Not only did my pastor teach the Word, but he taught us that holiness was how we could obtain eternal life. We were never allowed to make excuses for our poor decisions. He always challenged us to not only know the Word of God, but to also live the Word of God. Instead of feeding us the answer to the many questions we asked him, he always required us to search the scriptures for ourselves. Even though the process was time consuming, I enjoyed it. It required me to learn the different books of the Bible. I discovered that it was possible for this mysterious book to become familiar to me.

With every lesson, I grew. There had been things and habits that I instantly lost the desire to do. It seemed as if my mind started to switch on its own. I started to regulate my behavior and my thought processes without even realizing it. I developed a great desire to please God. I wanted to experience His presence as much as possible. For the first time in my life, I wanted to surrender to Him. I knew I needed to surrender every area of my life to have Him. The only problem was I didn't know how.

One of the first steps I took was getting baptized. That morning, I was a complete wreck. I was excited and nervous at the same time, yet I didn't truly understand why. I knew being baptized was not the final step I needed to take, but I knew it was a major step for me. As a result of God knocking on my heart, I decided that I wanted to truly live for Jesus without excuses. Even though I wasn't sure how to do it, I knew I wanted to.

On the day of my baptism, I stood on the shore of the lake listening to the scripture being read to me. Everything slowed down. I could feel my heart beating rapidly in my chest. I could hear every time I swallowed. I kept repeating the phrase, "new creature" over and over again in my mind. I kept telling myself, "Today I will be new. Today I will change. Today I will never be the same again." I knew my life would change. I felt deep down in my belly something would happen. I was scared yet excited with the unknown.

Even though I didn't know how my life would turn, I expected it to get better. My life seemed perfect at that point. The issues I had been experiencing with Maurice's ex had subsided. I was convinced that life would be more fulfilling serving Jesus. I believed that serving Jesus would be better than the lifestyle I had been living.

That afternoon, I bravely took the walk towards Pastor Holland in the middle of the lake. When I reached Pastor Holland, he encouraged me with scripture. I listened without truly hearing him. I had been too focused on the thought of making all necessary changes to truly serve God. My thoughts were abruptly interrupted by Pastor Holland instructing me to place my hand over my nose. Instantly he, with the help of his assistant, submerged me under the water. When I emerged from the water, I lifted my hands up as tears ran down my face. I cried tears of pure joy. My spirit rejoiced. I had taken a step in the right direction.

CHAPTER 16: THE GATES OF HELL BROKE OPEN

Whenever I made the right decision, I always experienced good in return. I thought that this was the way things were supposed to go. This false sense of reality was quickly shattered after I was baptized and decided I was going to live for Jesus. It was as if the gates of hell broke open in my life. I immediately started to experience obstacles in almost every area of my life. My perfect life turned into a nightmare.

My relationship with Maurice was exposed for what it truly was—a complete lie. Prior to being baptized, there had been a veil over my eyes. The "perfect" man I had grown to love was the worst man I had ever encountered. Rumors that Maurice had in fact gotten his ex pregnant for a second time resurfaced. When I heard it, I initially thought it was just another tactic she was using to interfere with our relationship. I thought it was a lie, but I still asked Maurice about. Maurice brushed it off and accused her of lying again. Without solid evidence, and because I wanted to appear supportive, I said nothing more.

As the days and weeks went by, evidence started to appear. There were odd phone calls at random inappropriate hours. There were deleted text messages. She appeared to have a small baby bump. I didn't know what to think at this point. Had it been another man's baby? Or even worse, was she carrying *my man's* baby? I didn't know who to believe. Maurice said it wasn't his baby because he had not slept with her, while she claimed it had been Maurice's baby. I was faced with a terrible choice. I could believe his ex and risk losing him, or I could believe him and pray that he was telling the truth. I made the only decision I could make—I believed him and prayed for the best.

Shortly after the rumors surfaced, Maurice accepted an opportunity to play semi-pro basketball in Tennessee. I was a little relieved to have him in another state; I was able to fully focus on me. I didn't have to worry about facing the rumors. I placed the uneasy rumors and thoughts I had in the back of my mind. I convinced myself that I had no reason to be insecure.

One evening, as I sat in my Constitutional Law class, my phone unexpectedly vibrated. I looked down and saw it was Maurice. I was confused as to why he would call me while I was in class. He knew my schedule. He knew I didn't like being interrupted during class or study time. I was committed to my routine. I silenced my phone and focused my attention back on the lecture.

During my break from class, I stepped outside to call Maurice. Prior to calling him, I noticed I had a voicemail from him. As I waited to hear the message he had left, my excitement grew. Lately, he had been leaving me sweet voicemails and sending me sweet emotion-filled text messages. I started to feel the same love as I had once felt for him before the drama and rumors surfaced. I sat there, looking out of a window, waiting to hear what he had to say. I could even feel butterflies fluttering in my stomach. As I listened to the message, the butterflies died—he had pocket dialed me.

I had no desire to listen to Maurice talk to another guy. I was about to delete the message, but then I heard a still, small voice within me tell me to listen. The voice stopped me dead in my tracks. I started the message over and listened. As I listened, I grew confused. Maurice was talking to another guy about a girl being "bad." My inner voice screamed, "Who's bad?!" The more I listened to him talk, I understood that he had been talking about another woman. From the bits and pieces I could gather from the conversation, Maurice had cheated on me with another woman.

After Maurice finished talking, I heard the unidentified male give him advice. He said "It's already out there. You're guilty. She has to decide if she'll accept it or not." After listening to the message several times, I called him. "I'm going to kill him," I thought to myself. He didn't answer. I left him a message and went back to class. I tried my hardest to pay attention to the lecture, but couldn't. I kept thinking, "he betrayed me!"

On my drive home, Maurice retuned my call. As I looked down at the phone, I hoped that he had a great explanation. I hoped that I heard things wrong. I really didn't want to face the music. I wanted my "perfect" relationship. I wanted to be in a relationship with someone who loved me just as much as I loved them. I interrupted my thoughts and answered Maurice's call. As he spoke, my hopes and desires were shattered.

Maurice had not only cheated on me, but the woman was pregnant. My heart broke in a million pieces. I asked him who she was. After a long pause, he told me that the woman whom he claimed was his "best friend" was pregnant. I was shocked. She was the same person who had spoken evil of me for what appeared to be no reason. I became sick. I couldn't breathe. I felt as if I was submerged under water and couldn't swim. My vision became blurred as I drove. My tears were like a blanket that covered my eyes. I cried hot tears that wouldn't stop. The pain I felt was worse than any pain I had felt in my life.

Nothing in my past had prepared me for the pain of betrayal. My entire body became numb because of the pain. His voice seemed far away. It's as if I blacked out for the remainder of the phone conversation. When I came to myself, I was in my apartment bagging up all of his belongings. I wanted every trace of him as far away from me as possible. After gathering all of his belongings up, I drove them to his mother's house.

I stood at his mother's front door with anger in my spirit and streams of dried tears on my face. After a few moments of me knocking, his mother opened the front door. She stood there smiling as she greeted me. When she saw my face, her smile disappeared. She had grown accustomed to my smile. She knew something was terribly wrong. She looked down at the large black trash bags laying at my feet. She asked me what was wrong. I looked at her and blurted out everything I had uncovered.

Maurice's mother stumbled backwards. Her eyes were open wide in disbelief. Her jaw dropped. She said, "hell no, she's not!" I told her she was and that Maurice had confirmed it. I continued speaking and told her that the only reason I had come over was to bring his belongings to her. She said she didn't want the belongings because he couldn't stay with her. Instead of taking the bags back to my car, I left them there and got the others.

When I was done dragging his belongings to her front porch, we talked. She told me that his "best friend" had recently came to her house. She said his best friend claimed to have been pregnant by her fiancé. The more I listened to his mother speak, the more disgusted I became. I became nauseous and light headed. Depression hit me.

That night, I cried myself to sleep. My apartment seemed cold and lifeless. Many questions ran through my mind. What had I done wrong? Was I not good enough? Why would he betray me? With each unanswered question, I felt weaker and weaker. The numbness I felt intensified. I felt as though I had been thrown into a horrible dream. No matter how hard I tried to wake up, I couldn't. I finally faced the music. This was my life. I wasn't dreaming. The man I loved cheated on me. The man I loved was having a baby with another woman. The man I loved betrayed me. My relationship was a lie and I didn't know what to do about it.

I told Maurice I couldn't be with him. I meant every single word. There was no possible way I could trust him again. The thoughts of him touching me turned my stomach and made my skin crawl. I deserved more than what he had given me. My mind had been made up. I was never turning back to him.

My singleness was short-lived. I believed I deserved better while my heart ached with pain that I had never felt before. I was completely torn. I felt alone and isolated. I couldn't openly talk about what had happened or how I felt because of shame and embarrassment. When I tried to open up to my friend Colbie, she boldly unapologetically told me, "He's whack and you deserve better." I knew it was true, but it hurt me more. When I told my friend Nikki, she cried with me instead of offering me advice. My sister Kamra was shocked, hurt, and upset, but she just listened. No one could give me a solution that would take care of both my heart and my mind.

I couldn't mentally make sense of the madness I was experiencing. Nights seemed longer, colder, and darker than usual. Days seemed as though they flew by. I had no appetite and was losing weight rapidly. The nice curves I had worked hard to gain were vanishing right before my eyes. The only thing that remained unaffected was school.

The pain and agony was too great for me to handle. I decided to get back into a relationship with Maurice. I knew at the time that was a gamble. I knew there was a possibility he wouldn't change. I prayed he would, but I knew only time would tell. Deep down, I hated myself for being so weak and giving in to him. I knew I deserved better. Every man I had been with in the past had treated me better than Maurice had.

While Maurice remained in Tennessee, I tried to heal. We communicated through text messages and by talking on the phone. He tried his best to reassure me every chance he got. His attempts were futile because I remained numb and depressed.

Shortly before Maurice returned, his first son had been born. Maurice immediately questioned the paternity of the child. The mother of the baby questioned the paternity, too. She had been in a relationship also when she slept with Maurice. The drama was too much for me to bear, but I continued to put up a strong front. I couldn't admit that I was dying inside. I couldn't admit the situation had gotten the best of me. I suffered in silence.

When Maurice returned from Tennessee, things were awful. Our relationship was strained. I tried my best to move forward but it was hard. I didn't trust him as far as I could throw him. I questioned his every move. My numbness intensified as the days went on. I regretted staying with him and wanted out, but I didn't know how to get out. I didn't know at the time we had a strong soul tie that kept me there. I wanted out, but my soul wanted to stay in.

My silent suffering was exposed without my permission one Sunday. As I hugged someone at church her body started to jerk violently. She instantly started to cry. She started praying and speaking in tongues. I stood there shocked and embarrassed at the same time. I felt like crumbling because I knew she was feeling my raw emotions. After a few minutes of her holding me and crying she told me my enemies were like thorns on my side. She continued to cry and speak in tongues. She then said "God said you won't pray to Him about it." I was stunned. It was true. I would pray to God on a superficial level. I wouldn't ask Him to help me get out of the situation because I got myself in. I felt like it had been my fault. How could I go to him and ask him to deliver me? She pleaded with me to ask God to help me.

Before she uttered those words I didn't know I could ask God for help with the mess I created. Later that night I prayed and asked God for help. I knew the situation I was in was more than I could handle. I knew I needed help in every area of my relationship with Maurice. I had been shacking and fornicating. I tried to do things on my own because I felt God wouldn't help me. I needed God to help so bad at that moment. I was barely hanging on mentally. Emotionally I was a wreck. I was losing weight and hair daily. I needed a Savior, so I prayed.

To calm the battle going on in my head, I flat out asked Maurice if he slept with his ex. To my surprise and horror, he admitted to it. The nightmare became even worse—he put my health in jeopardy, too. Maurice told me he went and made sure he didn't have anything. He had the nerve to say, "It could be worse. I could be telling you that you had something." I instantly wanted to murder him and bring him back to life only to murder him again.

I didn't know how to react. I was torn between love and hate. I felt as though I was with him by force. When he hugged me, my skin crawled. I wanted to vomit. I had no idea how I would get past the infidelity and the possibility that he had fathered children by two other women while he had been in a relationship with me. We had only been together for a little over a year and I had to face so much betrayal.

Our relationship suffered in every area. I had difficulty being intimate with him. I felt disgusted. My body screamed every time he touched me. I prayed for the encounter to be over. I stopped cooking for him. I refused to clean up after him. I only worried about myself. I felt like he didn't deserve everything I had done because he didn't appreciate me.

Shortly after returning home, his next child was born. Both mothers took paternity tests. Once the results came back, my world crumbled. Both children where his. I felt out of touch with reality. I knew I deserved better, but I couldn't force myself to leave him.

I accepted both children like I had accepted those before me. I can't tell you how I was able to get through the trauma I experienced. I can't tell how I was able to go on. I just did. Somehow, we were able to work on our relationship to the point that things started to turn for the better.

CHAPTER 17:MY WILDERNESS EXPERIENCE

I became stronger spiritually, mentally, physically, and emotionally. I grow closer to God. I continued to do well in school. I worked two jobs and interned. My life had stayed on course and improved despite the betrayal, drama, and pain.

During this process, I decided to abstain from sex. I wanted my life to line up with the Word of God completely. I became tired of feeling horrible when I had sex with Maurice. I loved him, but I loved God more. One night, I decided to talk to him about my concerns. I wanted nothing more at that point than for God to be pleased with my life. I wanted to dwell in God's presence as much as possible. Maurice acted as if he understood and was supportive of my decision to abstain until marriage. I was relieved.

A few days later, Maurice backpedaled. He started to pressure me by saying, "God knows our hearts. He knows we love each other." I tried my best to stand by my decision, but I always ended up giving in to his advances, only to regret it later. After picking myself up from my pit of sorrow enough times, I decided to stand by my pledge of abstinence. I refused to have sex with Maurice.

Maurice continued to unsuccessfully attempt to persuade me to have sex with him. I was beyond proud of myself each time I refused to sleep with him. In each instance, I felt as though I was taking a stand for Jesus. My body was being held as a vessel for God's usage only. For the first time, I no longer felt like a hypocrite. I felt good enough to serve God. I wasn't turning back to my old ways.

I continued to enjoy living a life totally surrendered to God without feeling bound. I was free to worship God and live boldly for Him. I felt like my life was on *high*. Then it happened. As we sat on my bed in our bedroom, Maurice proposed. I was shocked. I didn't think he was serious. I thought he was only proposing because he wanted to have sex with me. The proposal was random. He didn't even have a ring or money to buy a ring. It was not as I had imagined or hoped.

Maurice assured me he was serious. Though I was skeptical, I said yes. We had reached a healthy, happy point in our relationship. The drama we had experienced in the past wasn't looming over our heads anymore. Things had died down. Things had turned for the better. It made complete sense that the next step was for us to get married.

Against my better judgment, I started having sex with Maurice again. I attempted to justify what I was doing by telling myself that we were engaged to be married. I still felt guilty afterwards. I knew God wasn't pleased. I prayed that we would get married soon. I wanted to live all-the-way right. I wanted my lifestyle to be pleasing and acceptable in God's sight; I knew we would have to get married as quickly as possible.

Shortly after we became engaged, we visited my family in California. Everything about our trip was perfect. My family fell in love with him. We decided that we would start a family. I told my mother my plans. She immediately voiced her concerns and disapproval. I listened, but I didn't care. My mind was already made up. We were going to start our own family. We even agreed that we would get married in a small ceremony before I started to show.

When we returned home from our trip to California, we started trying to conceive. When I thought I was pregnant after trying to conceive, I picked up the phone and scheduled an appointment. At my first doctor's appointment, I was heartbroken. The pregnancy test I took was negative, but the STD test I took was positive. The shock and embarrassment debilitated me. The doctor knew how excited I was about the possibility of pregnancy. We both hoped I was. When my results came in, she couldn't even face me—she sent the nurse in to hand me a bag of condoms and my prescription.

I was humiliated beyond belief. How could he have cheated on me again? When did he cheat on me, and with who? I was lost for words. When I got in the car that evening, I boldly asked him if he cheated on me again. With a surprised look on his face, he swore he hadn't. He claimed that he had learned his lesson. I told him that he needed to go get tested.

That night, the doctor at the ER was on Maurice's side. He tried to convince me someone could contract trichomoniasis from the environment. I wanted to punch the doctor in the face. He had no right to give his opinion beyond medical information. He didn't know Maurice was a proven cheater. I was outraged.

I couldn't face the fact that Maurice had cheated on me and then proposed; I didn't want to believe he was that evil. I didn't want to have to tell everyone the engagement was off because he cheated. I allowed my pride to get the best of me as I turned a blind eye. I forced myself to believe the second doctor's report.

A few days later, Maurice had the audacity to question me. He asked me if I had been unfaithful. I was confused and upset that he would question my fidelity. I had always been faithful to him. So many things went through my head. I wanted to curse him out, but I didn't want to seem guilty. I wanted to break down crying, but didn't want to seem weak. Instead of doing any of that, I remained calm and told him that I hadn't cheated. I reassured him that I loved him.

A month after the first negative pregnancy test, I became sick with a fever. By that time, I still hadn't had my period. I visited urgent care to figure out what was going on. I didn't feel like my normal self. That evening, the doctor took my temperature and confirmed that it was elevated. After noting my other symptoms, she asked me to take a pregnancy test. I agreed to take the test even though I didn't think it was necessary.

After waiting for what seemed like forever, the doctor came in. She told me that I was in fact pregnant. I was shocked, stunned, and excited all at once. I was truly amazed. I was having a baby!

I couldn't wait to tell Maurice that we were having a baby. After I was given my discharge papers, I rushed to the car where he had been waiting. Once inside, I told him I was pregnant.

"Are you serious?!" He asked, smiling from ear to ear.

"Yes!" I replied.

We kissed and embraced. We both were excited. We were actually having a baby.

As soon as I calmed down, I reached for the phone. I had to tell my mother. Even though she wanted me to wait until marriage, I had to tell her. As I waited for her to answer the phone, my heart raced. I hoped she wouldn't be dramatic and angry. I prayed she would be excited.

Once she answered, I blurted out, "Guess what? I'm pregnant!" I held my breath as I waited for her response. I could tell she was smiling as she spoke. She was excited! We couldn't believe that becoming a mother was actually a reality for me. After 28 years of being childless, I was finally with child.

My first trimester was pure heaven. Maurice attended all doctor appointments with me. He woke up in the middle of the night to fetch my every craving. He never complained or got upset. Everything was perfect. Our baby was perfect. My little world seemed perfect.

Unfortunately, things were far from perfect. Maurice suddenly decided that he no longer wanted to have a small ceremony. I felt crushed and betrayed. I felt as though he had trapped me. I would have never agreed to start a family with him if I had known he would change his mind. I felt as though I had been set up. Maurice knew I wouldn't have stayed in Michigan after graduation unless I was married. To me, love was not enough to leave my family and friends for a boyfriend. Maurice knew I didn't want children out of wedlock. When he told me how he felt, I was sure he knew his intentions all along. He lied and I was stuck. I didn't want to raise a child without the father. I swallowed my feelings and accepted the reality.

One night during my third month of pregnancy, the unimaginable happened. Maurice woke me up.

"I can't do this anymore," he admitted.

"What do you mean you can't do this anymore?" I retorted.

"I don't want to be in a relationship anymore," he responded.

I wanted to vomit, yet I was overcome by numbness. He purposely got me pregnant and now he didn't want to be in a relationship. I was in disarray. How could anyone be so cruel? This time, I didn't try to convince him otherwise. I allowed him to leave.

When I heard the door close behind him, I laid on the couch. I was baffled. I didn't understand what had just happened. Things seemed unreal. I considered everything and couldn't detect any signs. He had been happy. He had shown no noticeable changes prior to the moments before we went to bed that night. He acted a little weird, but I didn't think much of it because I knew he was tired.

Once Maurice reached his mother's house, he called me. I wasn't ready for the bombshell he was about to drop on me. He told me that he was having a baby by another woman.

"What do you mean?" I asked in bewilderment. This time, it wasn't one of the other baby mothers. I couldn't believe my ears.

That morning, I sat and listened to him paint the gruesome picture of how another unfamiliar woman was pregnant. Maurice told me that they had met up prior to our trip to California and had sex. My jaw dropped.

"Who is this girl?" I asked.

"The female we had an argument about last year," he confessed.

He claimed that she was a friend that he grew up with, but I knew he was lying. I felt in my gut that there was something more. I sensed their attraction to one another. During that argument, I told him he could leave to be with her. He swore up and down there was nothing going on and even stopped talking to her. I was devastated to hear that he slept with her. I didn't know how to respond. I hung the phone up and sobbed.

I cried so much that my stomach started to heavily contract. I couldn't stop crying. The pillow I laid my head on was soaked with my tears. My face felt swollen and hot. I laid there praying and crying until I fell asleep. Once I woke up, I cried more as I laid in fetal position gripping my stomach. My stomach continued to contract. Fear enveloped my entire body as I wept. I knew I needed to calm myself because the baby was being affected. I knew I needed to pull myself together, but I didn't know how. I was pregnant with Maurice's child. He had decided he didn't want to be with me anymore, and another woman was also pregnant by him.

I never wanted to be a single mother. I made sure I protected myself and used birth control so I wouldn't become pregnant. I was livid that Maurice, someone I trusted, betrayed me. I didn't want to stay with him after finding out he had not changed. I knew I deserved better, but I was terrified of being a single mother. I didn't want what happened to me as a child to happen to my child. Out of fear, I decided to work things out with him.

The remainder of my pregnancy was difficult. After finding out another woman was also carrying Maurice's child, I became severely depressed. I felt as though I was trapped in a horror movie without an escape. I couldn't hide how I felt. During one of my doctor's appointments, my doctor lectured me on the importance of taking care of myself both physically and emotionally during my pregnancy. It was obvious that something was wrong with me. Out of concern, the doctor prescribed me antidepressants. I wasn't comfortable taking the medication, but I took the prescription anyways.

As I stood in line at the pharmacy, I texted my sister Kamra. I needed someone to get me out of taking the pills. I was torn. My mind told me not to take the pills, but the doctor assured me that the pills were safe for the baby. I didn't know what to do. After giving the prescription to the pharmacist, I waited anxiously. I sat in the waiting area praying as I texted my sister. After doing research herself, Kamra begged me not to take the pills. In the mist of the back-and-forth texting, my name was called to the pickup window. I retrieved my prescription and shoved the white bag of pills in my purse. I still hadn't decided what I was going to do. I stopped texting my sister and called her. When she answered the phone, I could hear the concern in her voice. I felt guilty. She made me promise that no matter what, I wouldn't take the pills. After a few seconds, I made the courageous decision to throw the pills in the trash.

I knew my emotional and mental state had an impact on my unborn baby. I didn't want to harm my baby, so I put my big girl panties on. I prayed a lot during that time. I repented for all my sins. I read my Bible more. By the grace of God, I managed to get through.

Though I had been experiencing the hardest time of my life, I managed to continue to do well in school. My sleepless nights didn't affect my attendance; I even continued to maintain honor roll. I knew it all was by the grace and mercy of God that I was able to persevere. Despite everything I had experienced during the last three years, I was preparing to graduate from law school.

In January 2012, I graduated from law school with honors while being seven months pregnant. I was amazed at the strength I had displayed. I managed to achieve one of my biggest goals while fighting for my sanity. I could have given up during the journey, but I didn't. I could have taken time off, but I didn't. No matter how much my mind had been attacked, I was able to push through and study.

My mother and sisters flew from California to attend my graduation. It was the first time since 2008 that we had all been together. It was the first time in years I had been around people who truly loved me for me. They had no ulterior motives. There were no hidden agendas. They were simply there to celebrate, uplift, and love me. That day, I felt free.

Post-graduation, I continued to work. I also enrolled in an L.L.M.—masters of law—program. I wasn't ready to take the bar exam, but I knew I had to do something. I needed to stay focused to maintain my sanity until my baby girl arrived. I needed to support myself and prepare for my baby.

As I waited for the arrival of my baby, Maurice's third son was born. By this time, I had learned how to disassociate. When Maurice told me he was born, I felt nothing. In fact, the only thing I felt those days were the kicks from my baby, the presence of God, and excitement about my future as an attorney. I no longer felt when it came to anything associated with Maurice, because my feelings towards him had grown too extreme. I was exhausted by the moments of deep love, extreme hatred, and rage towards him. Ultimately, I decide not to feel for him at all. I built walls around my heart and disassociated.

On April 25, 2012, my baby girl Aaliyah made her debut. After waiting seven extra-long days past my due date, she graced us with her presence. She came out of the womb quietly. When I held her in my arms, my heart became alive again. She had a bright complexion and her head was stacked with a mass of black, curly hair. Aaliyah was sweet and peaceful. Her calm demeanor made the transition into motherhood painless and easy for me.

After I gave birth to Aaliyah, my own body turned against me. I fell into post-partum depression. During the months after her birth, I would wake up in the middle of the night scared something bad was going to happen. I couldn't understand what was going on with me. I wanted to go to the hospital because I felt unsafe. One night in particular, I woke Maurice because I felt so alone and afraid. I needed someone to support me. I needed someone to tell me I was okay. I just needed someone to be my strength. As I spoke, Maurice seemed to get annoyed with me. He became upset because he didn't know what to do. I regretted opening up to him. I felt worse than I did before talking to him. I vowed that I would never confide in him again.

From that moment forward, Aaliyah was my comfort. I put all of my energy into caring for her. I gave her all of my attention when I wasn't working or attending class. Aaliyah had become my world and my strength. She was my nearest family member. She was the perfect solution to my loneliness. With her there, I felt whole again.

During one of Aaliyah's doctor appointments, I learned that I could get a therapist. After receiving the information, I immediately called to schedule an intake appointment. At the intake appointment, I was assigned a therapist. Although I was nervous about opening up to anyone, I did. Our therapist came to our apartment a couple of times a week to sit with us. She made sure I knew how to care for Aaliyah. She answered each and every question I had. She helped me to release some of my bottled-up tension. She had truly been a God-send. She genuinely cared about my mental and emotional wellbeing. She even supported my decision to overcome depression without antidepressants.

Although I knew I could be medically assisted with my depression, I refused treatment. Over time, I built strong faith in God. I knew He could heal me if I kept praying. I knew it would happen in a matter of time. I continued to attend church with Aaliyah. I even had someone come to my apartment once a week to study scripture with me. For the first time, I had a support system around me. I had a therapist who believed in me, a woman who was walking with me spiritually, and Aaliyah.

Maurice was not supportive during this time. He quit both of his jobs to pursue his dream of playing professional basketball. I was left alone to care for five month old Aaliyah. Aside from a few occasions, Maurice's mother didn't help much. By that time, I no longer had a relationship with her. I grew to distrust her. She had been a source of pain. In the early stages of my relationship with Maurice, I had grown to love her. I would spend hours at her house. When Maurice was away in other states, I would still spend time with his family. I respected her, enjoyed her company, and appreciated her dearly. She seemed to be easy to talk to and always appeared to be loving and warm towards me. I was drawn to her and grew to trust her.

As time went on, my trust for her grew. I eventually confided in her when I was going through the worst parts of our relationship. I told her what I couldn't tell my friends and own mother. She always encouraged me and validated my feelings. I had no reason to question her loyalty until others started to repeat what I had confided in her privately. I initially overlooked her gossip, but as time went on, I faced the music. Maurice's other children's mothers would find out things I had only told her. His family members would also repeat things she had told them. With each incident, I grew weary of her. By the time Aaliyah was born, I didn't trust her. I built walls around us, refusing to let her in.

While Maurice was away playing basketball, I became suspicious that I was pregnant again. My concern arose when I realized I had been craving sour candy like I had when I was pregnant with Aaliyah. I prayed it was not the case. Maurice and I had only been intimate a couple of times after the birth of Aaliyah. I didn't want to believe I was pregnant again. Aaliyah was only five months old at this time. I brushed my concern off as paranoia. I told myself it couldn't be the case since I was exclusively breastfeeding. I told myself God wouldn't give me another baby. I just couldn't be pregnant.

I went over every detail of the last few months after Aaliyah's birth. I discovered my postpartum depression had mysteriously disappeared. My eczema had become horrible again just like it had during my first pregnancy. I also carried a lot of weight I had gained during my pregnancy with Aaliyah. *No, no, no, no!* I thought. God would not do it to me. God knew I didn't even like Maurice. God knew I regretted having a child by him; I sure didn't want to have another baby with him. I prayed pregnancy away earnestly. I just *couldn't* be pregnant again.

The more I prayed, the more pregnancy symptoms I felt. I swallowed my fears and called to schedule an appointment. I prayed the entire drive to the doctor. I prayed as I sat in the waiting room. Everything around me slowed down. I felt as if the silence was too loud for my ears. I felt like I was a million miles away. My thoughts were interrupted when the nurse came in. She told me I was pregnant. I was estimated to be 10 weeks pregnant. I lost it. I told the nurse I needed them to retake the test. I told her over and over again that they made a mistake. I told her I couldn't have another baby.

The nurse allowed me to vent that morning. After I stopped, she calmly told me I was pregnant. She looked over at Aaliyah, who had been sitting in her car seat, and smiled. She told me everything would be fine; she could tell I was a great mommy. Shortly after she finished talking, I thanked her and left.

I waited almost a week to tell Maurice I was pregnant again. I had a lot of mixed emotions. I didn't want another child with him. I didn't think I could manage another child. I wasn't in love with him. I didn't want to be with him. I had swallowed my desires and stayed with him because I wanted Aaliyah to be raised in a two-parent household. I was devastated.

When Maurice returned home from Canada, I broke the news to him. He wasn't happy, and left for a few hours. I was shattered. That night, I told myself I would get an abortion. Prior to that night, I was against abortion. I had promised myself I would never get an abortion. However, I couldn't see myself having another child with him. I didn't want to be trapped any longer. I felt that the only option was to abort the baby.

I called my mother and told her I was pregnant again. My mother was shocked. She really didn't know what to say. At that moment, I didn't care what she had to say. My mind had already been made up. The more Maurice and I argued, the more I was convinced that having an abortion was the only option.

During this time, I grew angry at God. I stopped praying because I was ashamed to pray. I was going to have an abortion and that was that. I knew it was against God, and deep down I felt guilty, but I didn't care. God had given me another baby *knowing* my situation. I was convinced that God didn't care about me. I prayed for my relationship to get better and it didn't. I prayed for the rumors and lies to stop, yet they increased. I couldn't see God working, but He was turning things in my favor.

The few people who knew my plans to abort my baby tried to talk me out of it. My friend Nikki begged me to have the baby and give it to her while Colbie reminded me that God knew us before we were formed in our mother's womb. I couldn't get any support from anyone. I felt as though everyone opposed the future I planned for myself.

Not only were my family and friends against the idea, but so were the ultrasound techs. I had scheduled an appointment to find out exactly how far along I was immediately after finding out about the pregnancy. The morning of the appointment, I laid numb on the ultrasound table. I couldn't feel the cold gel the tech applied to my belly. I couldn't even hear the sweet coos from Aaliyah who sat near me. My mind was a million miles away.

I stared at the baby sitting comfortably in my womb. The baby looked huge. The ultrasound tech told me that the baby measured at ten and a half weeks. I couldn't believe it. How could I not have known I was pregnant? What was I going to do?

"I can't have the baby," I told the ultrasound tech.

"Why?" She immediately asked.

"I can't afford to have another baby. The baby's father isn't helping out. I have no support system. My family is in California." I looked over at Aaliyah, who was now sitting up playing with the other tech. *How could I take care of two babies? Where would the energy come from? How would I have enough love to give to two babies?* My thoughts were interrupted.

"There are programs in place to help you. If your baby is a girl, you can pass Aaliyah's belongings down…"

I laid there listening as I stared at the image of my baby. Suddenly, the baby turned its head and looked towards us. I was shocked.

I left the appointment knowing I had to have the baby. I sent the ultrasound picture to my mother, sister, and friends. Everyone was relieved when I told them I wasn't going to have an abortion. After making my announcement, I prayed to God. I repented for considering aborting the life He had given to me. I asked God to help me get out of the relationship I was in. I knew I didn't want the life I was living. I knew I deserved better. I knew my children deserved to have a better life—even if it meant being a single mother.

After praying, I waited for an answer from God. I didn't know what He would say or how He would say it; all I knew was that God had to answer this one prayer. I was desperately in need of direction. Shortly after I prayed, God answered. God told me to call my mother to ask to come home. Peace came over me. My mother always wanted Aaliyah closer to her. She had only seen Aaliyah twice. It made sense. I picked up the phone and called her. Once she answered, I asked if I could come home. With excitement in her voice, she said yes. I was certain that I was making the best decision for my children and I. I was moving back to California and I didn't care what anyone had to say about it.

I called Maurice and told him I was leaving. I told him I wasn't taking the children from him, but that I was doing what was best for them. He had moved to another state again to pursue his basketball career. He wasn't helping to support Aaliyah, so I didn't care what he had to say. I managed to support Aaliyah on my own up until that point. I could tell from his tone of voice that he wasn't happy, but I didn't care. I had enough. My mind was made up. There was nothing that he could say that would change it.

I knew that my relationship with Maurice wouldn't survive the move; I was okay with it. I was tired, I was hurt beyond repair, and I was ready to see what God had in store for me and my children. I was ready to be free.

For the next few months, I prepared to move back home in silence. I even kept silent about my pregnancy until five months in. During this period, it was confirmed time and time again that moving back to California was the best decision for us. Maurice's mother allowed the last woman he had a baby with to come around. I discovered that the women went with her to church, spent time with

114

her at her home, went to a birthday dinner, and even came to his grandmother's birthday dinner. I was humiliated by all of it.

I couldn't understand for the life of me why things happened as they did. I couldn't understand why Maurice's mother would allow the women he cheated on me with to freely come around. I felt betrayed and disrespected. I started to really despise his mother. I realized I could never win the battle I had been fighting, so I stopped fighting all together. I decided I would enjoy the remainder of my time in Michigan.

I found out I was having another baby girl. I had always wanted a daughter, and now God gave me two! I still didn't know how I would be able to be enough for two daughters. I had grown madly in love with Aaliyah. She had become my world. I wasn't ready to share what Aaliyah and I shared with another baby, but I knew that no matter how I felt, I had to press forward.

CHAPTER 18:BYE BYE, MICHIGAN

The time had finally arrived for me to leave Michigan. I managed to settle all of my affairs prior to leaving. There had been no complications. My transition was smooth and effortless.

Arriving to California was bittersweet for me. Prior to my arrival, my maternal grandmother had passed away. I was heartbroken. I loved my grandmother deeply. She was the best woman I had even laid eyes on. She was everything I wanted to be. Her compassion for others was limitless. She was a powerful prayer warrior. She lived a godly life in public and in private. Even though I was crushed by her passing, I had to hold myself together. I had to do what was best for my babies.

While I adjusted to my grandmother's passing, I adjusted to living at home with my family. It was extremely different for me. I had been away from home since I was 18 years old. I was no longer used to the many personalities. It was a major adjustment for me. I hated not having my own space, but l loved being around people who loved me.

After being home for a little over a month, we moved from Los Angles to Palmdale, CA. I was excited to be moving because it meant more privacy for me. Shortly after the move, Maurice flew to California. Even though I knew we would ultimately separate, I wasn't ready yet. We stayed together despite the fact that we weren't sure what would happen. I didn't want to be in a relationship with him, but I still wanted our daughters to grow up with their father.

On May 17, 2013, Myah Ra'nae was born. It took me a while to bond with Myah. I had grown completely numb to the world. I couldn't feel anything aside from the pain of depression. I looked in the mirror and couldn't identify with who peered back at me. I had just had another baby by the man I resented. I was constantly on edge and sleep deprived. I had moments of joy, but they were fleeting. I was being sucked into a black hole and I didn't know how to escape.

My faith in God was dwindling as the days went on. I completely stopped going to church. I started cursing again, yet it was worse than ever before. I was in full rebellion and I didn't care. I hated what had become of my life.

One sunny morning, things turned for the worse. I was using Maurice's phone to talk to my mother. Out of nowhere, text messages started to come through. I looked at the phone. To my horror, his children's mother was texting him. From what I could gather, they made plans to see each other when he returned home. I immediately told my mother I would call her back and kept reading the messages. As I read each message, I questioned him about the messages. Maurice started to lie. I handed him the phone and told him to unlock it. I wanted to see every message. He unlocked the phone and quickly deleted the messages. I was furious. We argued until I couldn't stand to hear his voice. I knew deep down in my heart Maurice was up to his old tricks, but I just couldn't prove it.

A couple of days later, Donnika and I went for a nice long walk while Maurice spent time with the babies. As I vented about what was going on, my sister remained silent. She seemed to become a little nervous. I asked her what was wrong. She told me a few days after Myah's birth, she heard Maurice on the phone with another woman. Initially, she thought he had been talking to me. But after several moments, she realized he wasn't talking to me. Maurice encouraged the other woman to not worry about her body because she only needed to work out to get it back. She described his tone of voice as being inappropriate. As I looked at her I could tell she was hurt.

My sister apologized for keeping the ugly truth from me. She explained that she didn't know how to tell me. I could tell she felt horrible. I was livid. As we walked back home, she begged me not to tell him. I lied and told her I wouldn't, even though I knew darn well I would. When we returned home, I went off. Maurice attempted to lie his way out of it, but I knew better. Maurice tried to avoid the conversation by walking out of the house. I walked out behind him. When I was tired of walking with him, I picked up the phone and called his mother. As soon as she answered, I told her I needed for her to send for him before he got hurt. After hanging up the phone with her, I went through the phone bill and discovered that Maurice had been talking to two of the other mothers every chance he got.

Two days after the incident, Maurice was preparing to leave California. Before he left, we sat on my grandmother's porch and talked. I wanted closure. We had grown beyond the dramatics by this point. I wanted to know exactly why he continued to lie. I wanted to know so that I could do things differently in my future relationships. As I sat there listening to him speak, I realized the truth—Maurice didn't care. The more he spoke, I accepted the reality there would never be a future between us. He would never be committed to me. He would never love me the way I deserved to be loved. I sat there motionless and numb as he explained how he didn't have a problem. He admitted he could stop carrying on inappropriate relationships with the other mothers at any time. I sat there listening to what he said and didn't say. There was no reassurance. He didn't say he crossed boundaries. He didn't apologize for his actions. I knew that he would never stop.

Once Maurice arrived back to Michigan, he continued living his life. He continued to speak without speaking. I continued to pay attention to the things he neglected to say in each conversation. The more attention I paid to the unspoken things, the more my desire to stay with him for the sake of our children died.

I saw Maurice once more that year after the death of his father. Even though he was with us in California, his mind and heart was in Michigan. At the time, I couldn't really understand what was going on. I didn't care to understand. I had been traumatized by him beyond repair. I knew he wasn't capable of loving me the way I needed and desired to be loved. I knew he wasn't the best for me. I just knew that trip was the last time Maurice and I would see each other.

Shortly after Maurice left, I started dreaming about him a lot. In one dream, I was sitting in a lounge area with other women looking out of a window. As I peered out of the window, I noticed Maurice on a basketball court playing with a team of guys. One of the women who had also been sitting in the lounge area expressed her interest in him. I became upset and told her we were engaged and had two children. The woman looked at me and told me she didn't care as she stood up and walked out of the lounge towards the basketball court. I was offended and angry. Before I could recover from that scene, the scene switched. I walked down a set of stairs into a living room where Maurice's mother and aunt had been sitting. I interrupted their conversation to tell them what had occurred in the dream. As I spoke, they just stared. They weren't concerned.

When I woke up from the dream, I cried. My heart was broken. I felt every ounce of pain, just as if the dream was real. I prayed and asked God what it all meant. "Leave him," God replied. That morning, I told Maurice about the dream. "I had a similar dream too," Maurice said. I never asked him the details of the dream because I didn't care. He reassured me that everything would be fine. He told me I shouldn't worry. Deep down, I knew something was seriously wrong. I knew Maurice was lying and cheating again.

I continued to have dreams. God continued to instruct me to leave Maurice. I knew I needed to leave him. I wanted to leave him, too. I just didn't have the courage or strength to do it. I knew something drastic had to happen. My dreams kept coming. God kept telling me to leave him. I kept ignoring God's voice until one Sunday during his sermon, my Pastor stopped dead in his tracks to say, "God said he's not going to open another door for you to bless him." I cried instantly. I knew God was talking to me. I felt as if a knife had been stuck in my heart.

I knew the message was for me because no matter how much I tried to move forward, doors wouldn't open for me. At that time, I was receiving public assistance with three degrees. I had applied to many jobs without any success. My mother paid my rent and bought whatever I couldn't buy with public assistance. I knew God wasn't pleased with my disobedience. I knew I couldn't continue to live the way I had been living. I knew I needed to leave Maurice even though I thought my heart wasn't strong enough.

I prayed for strength daily. I prayed for courage. I prayed to God for exposure even though I knew what the dreams meant. I knew something was going on because Maurice had been unavailable when I called him. He wouldn't return my calls or text messages for hours and he started speaking harshly towards me. After being pushed to a breaking point, I boldly asked him if he was cheating. He replied "no." I knew he was lying, so I checked my phone bill. I discovered Maurice had been talking to someone as I had expected. I questioned him about it again the next day. He said she was nothing to worry about because he was with me. I was disgusted. I kept looking through the phone bill. I discovered his "situationship" started shortly after he returned to Michigan in November 2013. I grew numb. I had no tears to cry this time. I called him but he didn't answer. I left him a message and told him I was done. After 4 years and 10 months, I finally had enough. I finally decided to let go of man and trust God.

CHAPTER 19:MY REDEEMER WAS MY PROTECTOR

After leaving Maurice, I braced myself for the worst. I expected to feel a tremendous amount of pain and an overwhelming amount of hurt. I had been in a relationship with him for 4 years and 10 months. Maurice had been a big part of my life. Though our relationship was filled with hurt, pain, betrayal, and one-sided love and commitment, it still existed. To my surprise and disbelief, there was no pain. I never felt a moment of hurt. The withdrawals I thought I would experience were nonexistent. I didn't miss him one bit. I felt completely free for the first time in a while. It was as if God had held my heart as He shielded it from any more pain.

Two short weeks after I broke off the relationship with Maurice, God revealed His will for my life to me. As I slept one night, I had a dream. In the dream, I saw a side view of a male. He had been looking at something or someone. As I watched him standing there, wearing a white tuxedo jacket with black trim, God whispered to me, "that's your husband." I woke up confused. I had no desire to be in a relationship with anyone. I had just escaped the death trap of a relationship I had been in. I wanted no part of being with anyone. I brushed the dream off.

Three nights later, I had another dream. This time, I found myself peering at a little, round-faced, curly-haired boy. As I watched the sun reflect off of his smooth, tan skin, I heard God say, "that's your son." I woke up from that dream knowing it had been from God. I had no desire to have another child. I was content with my daughters. But because God said I would have another one, I accepted it.

My single season was the start of a new chapter in my relationship with Christ. For the first time in my walk, I was mentally free. I was at a place where God could really teach and guide me. My heart was no longer torn. I no longer had to choose between pleasing God and pleasing a man made of dust. I finally made the decision to commit my life to Christ without holding anything back.

Less than two weeks after leaving Maurice, God opened the first door for me. I had tirelessly searched for a job without success. No matter how I would revise my resume, no one wanted to hire me. I knew I was overqualified, but I needed a job to support my babies. I was tired of being on public assistance. I was at a point where I was desperate and would take anything. Even though I was discouraged, I kept applying because I had faith that something had to come through.

After applying for several more jobs, I received a job lead. My brother Jacob had been working as a transporter. He encouraged me to apply to his job. I applied and hoped for the best. After a couple of days, I received a call that I had been hired. Even though I would be making minimum wage and would have to travel on a train and two buses, I was beyond excited. At that point, I was willing to work anywhere as long as it meant working to providing a better life for my daughters.

To help with my transition from home to work, Donnika watched my children. I was relieved. I didn't have to worry about my babies being mistreated. I didn't have to worry about waking them up before the sun rose to take them to daycare. Donnika took great care of them. She treated them as if they had been her own, and she was compensated for the hours she cared for them. God had literally worked out every single detail. I was grateful.

I commuted from Palmdale to Los Angles at least three times a week for work. The commute took over three hours each way. Most mornings, I had to wake up at 3 a.m. to catch the first train. Once I arrived in Los Angeles, I took two buses to work. It was during these early-hour commutes that I was able to spend the most time with God. After getting on the train every morning, I would pray for revelation, knowledge, wisdom, and discernment before reading a few scriptures. Afterwards, I would fall asleep. Over time, I had a clearer understanding of God's word. Eventually, I found myself reading the Bible for the majority of the train ride. I started to delight in the Word of God. I could feel God wash me with His word. Day by day, the scriptures came alive.

The person I once knew started to resurface. I found myself laughing again. I was able to provide for my children and felt confident once again. The numbness I had grown accustom to vanished into thin air. The extra weight I gained fell off. For the very first time in years, my mind was truly at peace. And it was all because God had pushed me down a path I was too afraid to walk down.

I was grateful for the opportunity I had been given, but I wanted much more than what I had. I wanted to work closer to home. I wanted to make more money so that I could get off of public assistance completely. I started to apply for jobs again. I had only received a couple of job offers which weren't a fit for my life. I kept applying and praying for another door to open. The more I applied, the more opposition I felt. I started to feel defeated again. I felt as though God had turned a deaf ear to me and I didn't understand why. I was serving Him in spirit and truth. I expected Him to give me what I wanted, but He didn't. I was confused.

One night, I vented to Colbie about my frustrations. Instead of validating my feelings, Colbie shared her perspective. She told me I had to be content in my current season. She shared with me how God kept doors closed for her for over a year when she wanted to change jobs. She expressed how frustrated she had become until she decided to take things one day at a time. She said she would tell herself every day she remained at that job that it was the day that God decided she would still be there. She expressed how grateful she had been for the time God kept the door closed. It was there, the job she wanted to leave, that she met her husband.

After prayer and Colbie's encouragement, I stopped applying for jobs. By then, my application total had reached 91. I realized God was not opening any doors for a reason. No matter how badly I wanted to leave the job, God didn't want me to leave just yet. As difficult as it was to do, I forced myself to become content where I was until God decided to place me somewhere else.

I decided to work as unto the Lord. Even though I only made $8.00 an hour, I worked as if I made a million dollars an hour. I continued to arrive to work early. I remained kind and polite to everyone even though customers and management treated us like servants. I read so much Word that it became a part of me. I was changing from the inside out. I was tested and tried, but was able to stand because of the word that flowed from my belly. God's word had become my comfort and guide while I worked as a transporter.

I spent many nights reading the Bible. Instead of picking up the remote and watching reality TV or listening to music that would feed my silly emotions, I read. I started to hear God speak to me through His word. I found myself getting lost in scripture. I grew more and more in love with Christ the more I read. The barriers and assumptions that I adopted from religion were replaced with true relationship. I was totally surrendered to Jesus and I loved every second of it.

Through my submission to the Word of God, I learned how to fervently pray and worship. Even though I prayed before, something different was now happening during my prayer time. Each night I cried out to God, I started to feel His presence more and more. I found myself getting lost in the warmth and sweetness of His spirit. My bedroom would start off cold as worship music played softly. As I praised and worshipped God's holy name with lifted hands, His glory would come in. His presence was unexplainable. Everything I had ever wanted I had in that moment. The intimacy I wanted with my Savior I had. I would pray and cry out until His Spirit released me. I found the strength I needed from His presence. In His presence I found peace, joy, and deliverance.

The chains that kept me bound started to break in His presence. In worship services, I would feel the breaking in my spirit. As my Pastor preached, I felt burdens lifting off of me. I started to feel light and unbound. I was amazed and in awe because of everything. God was shaping and molding me by His very presence. God was delivering me as I stood in His presence day by day.

The tighter I clung to God, the stronger I became. I no longer resented my mother for allowing me to be molested. I no longer resented my father for abandoning my life. I no longer resented Maurice for the hell I endured while being with him. My perspective of being a single mother of two small children changed. I started to fall in love with the reflection I saw looking back at me. I started to believe in her again. I knew she was capable of being who God called her to be. I became fearless again. I became an overcomer.

In September 2014, I started to dream about numbers and open doors. Initially, I tossed the dreams to the back of my mind. I didn't know what they meant because I had never dreamt numbers before. I had never dreamt about doors being unlocked. I didn't think they held any significance until a woman of God explained that numbers had significance. That night after speaking to her, I decided to research the numbers in my dreams. After about an hour of research, I understood the dreams had much significance. I was coming out of the season I had been in.

When I went to church the following Sunday, God dropped more revelation about my dreams on me. The sermon's theme was, "you're coming out of your current season." That day, I praised God like never before. I praised the Lord almost like David had praised the Lord when they carried the Ark of the Covenant. I had danced intensely because my spirit received the revelation; I knew what was about to manifest in the natural.

Several days after my David experience, I received an unexpected phone call. The person was a representative for Los Angeles County Department of Children and Family Services. She extended me an invitation to interview. I had interviewed with them for the same position a few times without any success. By this time, I had grown used to interviewing, getting excited, and being hopeful only to receive no call back. But this time, I felt a difference in my spirit. I couldn't understand why, so I told myself to calm down. No matter how much I tried to calm my spirit, it rejoiced even louder.

The morning of the interview, I prayed. I tried to be as calm as possible, but my spirit danced like it had never danced before. It was uncontrollable. I found my limbs dancing and praising God after a while. I danced and praised as I got ready for the interview. I didn't understand what was going on, but I knew something was happening in the spirit realm. The praise was so contagious that Aaliyah joined in. As I danced, I decided to anoint my tongue, my hands, and my feet by placing the oil directly on their surfaces.

As I sat in the interview, I had peace. I wasn't intimated by the faces of the five Assistant Regional Administrators (ARA) that were in front of me. I answered every question thoroughly. I asserted myself and allowed God to flow through me. I left the interview that day knowing that no matter what happened, I would be just fine because God's will would prevail.

Two days later, as I drove from one location to the next, I received a voice message from an unfamiliar phone number. After listening to the message, I realized it had been one of the ARAs. I could tell from the sound of her voice it had been good news. I calmed my spirit and nerves before retuning her call. She told me she had been very impressed with my interview and wanted to personally offer me the position. I was ecstatic! I quickly thanked her and accepted the position. Immediately after hanging up the phone, I had a praise break in the car. No longer would I have to commute far to work! I would finally be able to fully support my children without the help of public assistance! I would be able to provide them with medical coverage! I wouldn't have to work weekends or holidays!

Even though the position was not a position in the legal field, it was perfect. What I once brought home all month, I made in one pay period. The job wasn't stressful. It was perfect for the season I was in. I no longer had to wear one-dollar flip flops or black Bruce Lee shoes because I could now provide for the girls and for myself. More importantly, the position enabled me to pay for and take the bar exam.

Six months after working in my new position, I decided it was time for me to move into my own place with the girls. I loved my family, but I needed to break away. I had been on my own for many years prior to 2013. I was used to being independent. Even though I loved my sister, I wanted to be separate from her, as well. I wanted to create the home environment that I wanted without outside influences. However, at the last minute, I decided that it would be better for my sister to move with us.

After looking at a number of places, we found the perfect home. Initially I was nervous; my credit wasn't that great because of my season of unemployment. I knew my sister's credit wasn't high, either. I wanted that townhouse badly. It was the only place that felt like home. To my surprise, not only were we approved based on credit, but we qualified for the lowest deposit payment. We praised God because we knew it was because of Him. He opened that door for us. I was blown away! As I praised Him, God reminded me that the townhouse was the exact place I had desired to live in a year prior.

We moved into our townhouse August 1, 2015. I saved enough money for furniture and appliances. I felt as though nothing could stop us. After being in California for a little over two years, we finally had our own place to call home!

Our first night in our new home was uncomfortable for me. I could barely sleep. I found myself watching Aaliyah and Myah as they slept in their own beds. They were sleeping peacefully, but I was worried. I had grown accustom to sharing a room with them. Before that night, I thought I wouldn't have an issue not having them in my bed. I thought I was ready for them to get out. I thought I was ready to have a bed to myself for the first time in years, but I wasn't. Though it was hard, I managed to adjust and get comfortable in our new home.

I knew I was able to enjoy the comforts of my own home because of God. He had opened the door nine months prior for me when He landed me a new job. He made a way for me to get approved for the townhouse. I was extremely grateful. I no longer had to worry about the insect infestation we were forced to deal with in the previous place. Not only were my new neighbors clean, but the townhouse complex was clean, also. I no longer had to worry about the issues I faced living with male family members. I didn't have to worry anymore about anything but taking care of my babies, working, and loving Jesus.

Without warning, my carefree bubble burst. Donnika decided she wanted to spread her wings and fly. After visiting her boyfriend in Tennessee, she decided that she wanted to live there. I was both shocked and furious. My sister had been Myah's nanny ever since she turned 9 months old. I had grown comfortable with her constant presence in their lives. The stress of single motherhood was not felt because Donnika had been a huge comfort and support for us. I felt like my entire world was crumbling. I had no backup plan because she had always been there. I cried and prayed for direction. My mother came to my rescue for a few days by taking the girls to her house while I worked. I knew I needed to do something, but I just didn't know what.

After speaking to my mother and other mothers, I decided I needed to snap out of my shock. The first step I took was locating a learning center for my babies. I didn't want to do it, but I had no choice. After speaking to a coworker, I located the perfect center. I completed all of the necessary paperwork and visited the center at random times over a three day period. I talked to staff members and observed how they interacted with the children and how the children interacted with them. I prayed and prayed before making my final decision.

The following Monday, my daughters were introduced to their new environment. Myah had a difficult transition while Aaliyah flourished. We had kept Myah close to us at all times because she cried a lot. Even though she was two and a half, we still held her close. Donnika spoiled her to tell you the truth. As a result, when she went to the learning center she had a very difficult time. Myah wanted her teacher to pick her up, but she couldn't. There were other little children in the class room who needed attention as well. There were other activities the teacher needed to tend to. With all of the obstacles, Myah's teacher still went above and beyond to help her transition. She allowed Myah to hold on to her leg all day if she wanted to. Myah stayed close to her teacher until she became comfortable, confident, and was well-adjusted.

We all managed to adjust to the change rather quickly. We missed my sister, but we enjoyed the change. One day as I drove down the street, God explained to me why He allowed things to happen as they had. He had to remove my sister because I had been relying on her more than I had relied on Him. I was stunned. I couldn't argue back or deny it because it was true. I always knew my sister would help me with whatever I needed her help with. She loved the girls and took great care of them. I always assumed she would be with us. I never considered her plans for her own life. Once again, I realized that I tried to plan her life for her. With God's revelation, I was able to let go of the bitterness I carried against her for leaving me without warning. She had every right to live her life the way she wanted.

As the months went on, I started to struggle financially. I didn't anticipate it would be so difficult taking care of my daughters and living completely alone. Their father didn't support them financially. My mother wasn't in the position to help financially, and even if she had been, I would not have asked. I wanted to support my little family on my own.

Instead of talking about my financial problems, I prayed to God. There were nights I would cry myself to sleep because my stomach had been empty and my heart ached. During this season, I would eat little to nothing so that my children could eat as much as they wanted. I had never imagined I would be in this position. I was constantly late on my rent and grew afraid of being evicted. At that time, I was doing all that I could possibly do to stay afloat.

As broke and broken as I was, I found strength in God. He had become my everything. I had grown to know Him as my provider. Every time I would run out or was close to running out of food, God sent blessings my way. One year around Christmas, someone placed a gift certificate on my desk at work. That morning I looked in my refrigerator and noticed I wasn't going to have enough milk, cereal, or meat beyond a couple of days. I told God, "If this is a path you're taking me down, I will go." That morning, I went to work and started working as soon as I stepped in the door. I left my thoughts about the food not stretching at my front door. After returning to the office, I walked away from my desk. Once I returned, I found an envelope on my desk. I opened it and was astounded. Someone had given me a $100 gift certificate! I didn't even know who had done it. I quickly took the gift certificate and placed it in my purse before taking a walk.

As I walked around the parking lot, I tried to make sense of things. I tried to think of who could have done it. I couldn't understand how they knew I needed it. As I tried to figure it out, I started to cry. God did it again! I wouldn't know what it was to go completely without because He made a way. He touched someone's heart that day. I was able to go to the store and buy the things I needed. I even had some money left over.

Christmas that year was difficult. I didn't have any money for a Christmas tree or Christmas gifts. The little money I had was spent on bills and food. That year, I decided not to worry about Christmas. I wished I could have done more, but I understood that providing a home and food was most important. My mind was made up— Christmas was cancelled in my household. My children didn't know anything about Christmas besides Christmas lights. If I took them on a drive to see lights, they would be satisfied. I had everything figured out until a woman at my church approached me. She told me the church would be giving gifts for the children the upcoming week. I decided to swallow the little pride I had left. That week, I stood in line during my lunch break with everyone else. I waited for my turn to get toys for my children. I couldn't believe I was where I was. Though it hurt, I was grateful. My church had given my children Christmas just when I had decided to cancel it.

My blessings kept coming that Christmas season. My children were also given bikes from my church. My coworker gave me an artificial Christmas tree with bulbs and Christmas lights. I continued to remain silent about my situation and people kept coming with blessings. I didn't hint to anyone that I had been having severe financial problems, nor did I stop smiling. God continued to send everything I needed at the perfect time.

Being financially broke was not the only brokenness I felt. For some odd reason, my heart was broken. I would lay in bed or on my living room floor many nights crying. I didn't understand why my heart ached so much. I had not dated since I left my ex, but I felt as though someone smashed my heart. The pain was so severe at times that I became paralyzed. The only movement I felt would be the streams of tears that flowed uncontrollably from my eyes.

During that season, God would not allow me to reach out to anyone. Honestly, I didn't want to reach out to anyone, either. I didn't trust anyone with my problems. So, every single night I would cry and pray. Every time, I would cry as though a drought had been released. I cried all the pain I had felt in my life out during that season. At times, I felt as though my spirit wept for the little girl hidden inside of me. My spirit wept because I never had a father. It wept for the years my mother had gone missing to the streets. It wept for every broken relationship I experienced. My spirit wept so much because God decided it was its season to mourn.

With every tear I shed, I felt the weight of my past lifting off of my shoulders. With every tear, God placed my heart back together piece by piece. With every tear, years of pain were released. I cried until

God finished surgery on my heart. When He finished, I felt as though I went through an emotional master reset.

During this season, God taught me to not complain. My daughters were constantly growing out of clothes. I was always replacing things for them. Purchasing clothes for them all the time left me without any resources to purchase things for myself. Initially I was unbothered. I had enough clothes from the past. I thought I would be fine up until my shoes became worn to the point where I had holes in the bottom of them. To protect my feet from the cold or wet ground, I placed cardboard in them. As hard as it was to endure, I endured without complaining. I knew it was necessary. It was more important for my daughters to have shoes that fit than for me to have a new pair of shoes.

Even though I couldn't afford things for myself, I still praised God. I even danced for Jesus in those shoes. I never thought I would ever experience wearing shoes with holes in them. I never imagined I would still be as grateful to God as I had been. But I was.

My broken season lasted for over a year and a half. As hard as it was, I learned to truly praise God for Him being who He was. I appreciated Him for forming the earth. I was broken beyond belief, yet I had a praise on my lips.

In the midst of my brokenness, my spiritual gifts were awakened. I had never imagined I would speak in church, but I did. I had no desire to stand in front of anyone and speak about the Word of God. I felt like I wasn't equipped and or knowledgeable even though I had been studying the Word of God. Despite how I felt, God knew I was ready.

I stood in front of a group of women in church one night teaching on Hebrews 11. At the time, I didn't expect that researching the topic of faith would give me the tools I needed to get through that season. I needed to speak about faith. I needed a biblical foundation about faith because I would need it when the enemy came up against me. Faith was exactly what I had been walking in that season. Walking in faith was what was going to get me from brokenness to wholeness. My unwavering faith in God is what made me whole at the conclusion of that season.

CHAPTER 20:SEND ME LORD, AND I'LL GO

After ending my season of brokenness, I was a lot different. I no longer saw the world or even God the same. The things that would bother me in the past no longer bothered me. Instead of becoming angry and reacting out of anger, I would take my frustrations to the Lord in prayer. I became quick to forgive people and quick to overlook wrongs. I came out of the fire stripped of habits and ways I hadn't been able to break free from in the past. No longer did I send precious prayer time calling out my desires and issues. No longer did I petition Heaven with prayers about only my family.

I started asking God to equip me for His Kingdom. I would pray for God to show me how to love like He loves. I prayed for Him to show me what breaks His heart and to break mine, too. I wanted to be used for His glory and His glory alone. God taught me how to be more Christ-like. I no longer just talked about holiness and living righteously, I actually lived it.

It was during this time that my spiritual gifts started to manifest. I dreamed of events that came to pass. I wasn't left with questions regarding what I had dreamed. I started to have more clarity and insight. I actually understood what God was revealing to me. When I would pray, I saw visions flash before my eyes. It was as if I was dreaming while awake.

One particular dream changed the course of my spiritual life forever. My younger cousin Aysun ("Charde") had been battling cancer. When she was diagnosed, it had already progressed to stage four cancer. The doctors told her she would have to go through radiation treatment for a six month period. Three months into treatment, the doctors were astonished because her body scans showed no hint of cancer. We praised God because we knew God had healed her. He performed a miracle! Unfortunately, months later she was diagnosed with a different form of cancer. This form of cancer wasn't only rare, but it was also extremely aggressive. It hurt me deeply to see her suffer. She was like a little sister to me. We spent countless hours with each other growing up. Almost all of my favorite memories included her. When I dreamt about her dying, I was sick to my stomach. I recall waking up that night with a heart so heavy that I couldn't even function.

I knew my dreams foreshadowed what was to come. Every time I dreamt, what I saw came to pass. That night, I lay in my bed an emotional wreck. Aside from my grandparents and aunt, no one had passed away in my immediate family. I wasn't prepared to say goodbye to Charde. As I prayed, God let me know that there was nothing I could do to stop her from dying. This time, God didn't instruct me to intercede for her. His only instruction was to go to her and tell her she had to decide that day whether or not she was going to serve Him.

Three days after having the dream of Charde dying, God made a way for me to go to her. That day, my coworker needed a CD with X-ray images delivered to a hospital in Los Angeles. I offered to deliver it because I knew I needed to go speak with Charde. At that time, I didn't know she had been admitted into the very same hospital I was going to. I thought I would have to drive across town to see her on my lunch break. I was prepared to drive wherever I needed to drive to speak with her.

That morning after finishing my assignment, I typed the address into my GPS. I was shocked when it directed me to drive up the hill. At that moment, I knew God had set everything up. I almost instantly became anxious, nervous, and scared. My heart felt as though it was going to jump out of my chest. I knew whatever God had sent me to say was more than I had ever done before. In that moment, I understood that God meant business.

After parking, I walked across the courtyard of the hospital in the direction of where Charde was. People were everywhere. I could hear the noise bouncing from building to building that afternoon. I felt as though I had been a million miles away. I could feel the sun beaming on my face, yet I felt numb. As I walked, I prayed to God for help. I didn't know what He really wanted me to say. I knew I was not permitted to tell her that she was going to die. I knew what God would say through me would be important. I knew God needed me to be bold as a lioness because Charde's life depended on it.

When I reached her hospital room door, I paused before going in. That pause felt like an eternity. I took a deep breath as I grabbed the handle and turned it. I knew in that moment there was no turning back. I knew God was there with me because I could feel His Spirit resting on me. As I walked in, I heard the monitors beeping. I saw her laying in the bed fast asleep. My nostrils were instantly clogged with the scent of sterilization. My skin grew cold from the cool air streaming out of the air vent. I gathered all the strength and courage I had within me and whispered her name.

Charde had not expected to see me standing there that morning. I hadn't told anyone I was coming. As I approached her bedside, I whispered a little louder. This time, she woke up.

"Hey Roscoe, what are you doing here?" she said, puzzled.

Instead of answering her question, I greeted her back as I sat on the right side of her bed.

As I sat there, I heard myself speak even though I couldn't feel my mouth moving. I had an out-of-body experience and was watching myself. I could hear myself asking Charde for her hands before explaining to her why I had come.

"God loves you," I said obediently as I held her hands. "And I love you," I watched myself tell her. "I'm coming as a disciple of the Lord."

Instantly she looked at me seriously. She knew I meant business. At that very moment, I realized for the first time what my assignment was. After praying with her, God continued to word my mouth and speak through me.

"God said you have to decide today whether you are going to serve Him. He said you don't have until tomorrow. Today is the day," I uttered with urgency.

I saw tears fall from her eyes as I poured everything I had heard God say out. Every word was necessary.

Immediately after I finished speaking, I felt strange. I felt embarrassed. I asked myself why I said what I said. I even wondered where the boldness came from. I wanted to disappear, so I said good bye and left quickly. As I walked back across the courtyard, I became more nervous because I had to call her mother as instructed by God.

As I waited for my aunt to answer the phone, I prayed. I really didn't want her to answer the phone. I was afraid of what I had to tell her. God instructed me to tell her that her baby was going to die. He told me to tell her that our prayers had come up before Him. He heard our prayers for her healing, but now wanted to hear *her* prayers. He wanted me to remind her of what His word said. As I prayed, my aunt finally answered. As I spoke, she listened on the other end. When I stopped speaking, she thanked me. I was surprised to hear her thanking and praising God on the other end. She told me that she had been walking her floors that morning praying for the Lord to save her baby's soul. I was astonished.

Prior to my conversation with my cousin, Charde wouldn't listen to anyone who uttered God's name. She had become upset at God because she was battling cancer. Instead of enjoying her life with her two sons, she was in and out of the hospital. She was angry and I understood why. We all understood. As I stood there listening to my aunt, my heart broke. My aunt told me God had sent me because He knew she would listen to me. At that moment, I thought about our last outing before she became really sick. As we sat at the park watching our children play, Charde told me that God saved me so that the younger people in our family would have an example.

As I drove back to work that afternoon, I received a notification on my phone. Charde tagged me in a post. As my car stood still in traffic, I clicked the notification. As I read the post, my heart started beating fast. My cousin thanked me for coming to minster to her. She confessed that she had given her life to God. I couldn't believe my eyes! My body was covered with chills. I praised God and gave Him all of the glory. He used little old me in such a mighty way. All I could think was, "Lord, you are beyond amazing!"

My praises for God intensified as I read the comments left on the post. Charde's mother commented and asked her had she given her life to God before she posted on Facebook. My cousin's reply was, "yes." Her mother then commented she had seen rainbows on her living room wall. I started to cry. I knew God truly moved that day in my cousin's life. I knew that the covenant to save her soul had been sealed. The rainbows were proof. There had not been rain that day. The living room wall was not positioned near any windows. I knew that day all of Heaven rejoiced because she repented.

A month and a half after visiting Charde, I had another dream. In that dream, I saw her again. She was more beautiful than I had ever seen her. Her skin glowed. It was as if I was looking at glory. I had never seen anyone's face shine so brightly. When I woke up, God gave me direct revelation. My cousin's time was near. At that time, my cousin's health was quickly deteriorating. Her stature had grown frail. Her pretty brown skin was dull and lifeless. Her body was preparing for her transition from this earth.

Her parents assisted her in the transition. They prayed with her and held Bible studies at their home and in the hospital. They ushered her into the spiritual realm. My cousin started to delight in the Word of the Lord. She listened to worship music often. Even on her death bed, she requested her parents to read the Word of God to her and to play worship music.

Three short months after I went to her, she transitioned into her resting place. Even though our family was hit hard emotionally, we still praised God. The Lord had allowed her mother, step-father, father, brother, sisters, children, cousins, and aunts to be with her as she transitioned. Our family was allowed to see the full manifestation of God's glory through her. As she took her last breath, a glow fell upon her and peace surrounded everyone.

The next night after her passing, I struggled mightily. Everything that I spoke had come to pass. I wrestled with my spirit to the point that I would jump up when I felt myself falling asleep. I had known so much; I couldn't understand what God was doing in my life. I couldn't understand why people were saying what they were saying about the gifts I operated in. I couldn't understand why God would trust me with such important gifts. I begged God to change His mind concerning me that night.

The more I thought that night, the more I pleaded with God. My dreams always came to pass quickly. I walked up to strangers just about everywhere and told them what the Lord said. I cried as the thoughts escaped my mind. I was confused because I didn't understand what was going on with me spiritually. My confusion was lifted during a Sunday service when my bishop uttered "God said He's sending you to the nations," before laying hands on me.

From that moment on, I started to walk in the anointing God had given me. I was no longer afraid to tell someone what the Lord told me to say. I started to understand the purpose behind my spiritual gifts. People needed to hear from God even when they lacked an ear to hear. People need warnings before destruction. People need encouragement to know God sees and hears their prayers. God decided from the foundation of this earth that He would use me to speak into the lives of others. It took God to use me in my cousin's life for me to truly understand. From that moment on, I was no longer afraid of their faces. My attitude became, "send me Lord, and I'll go."

CHAPTER 21: WHEN DEVASTATION HITS

Ilearned to flow and accept what my life was becoming. I became more active in church and the Kingdom of God. I no longer complained about the 3 a.m. prayer sessions. I no longer depended on what I saw—I grew to rely on the things I could not see while moving in the natural.

As I increased spiritually, my finances started to increase, too. I was finally able to pursue my career goals again. I started to pursue my license as an attorney. I took the California bar exam and didn't pass. At that time, I was okay with it because I had expected to have some adversity. I had graduated from law school 4 ½ years prior to taking the exam. I was completely confident that I would pass on the second attempt. I gained an understanding of the exam's structure. There was no way I wouldn't pass the second time. For several months, I committed myself to studying for the upcoming bar exam. I refused to watch TV. I didn't go anywhere besides work and church. I knew as long as I put in the hard work, I would come out with the right results.

The day of the exam, I walked into the testing facility with confidence. I knew I had prepared for this round. As I approached the entrance door, I had a vision of me standing with my right hand raised taking the attorney's oath. I almost broke down crying because I felt I had received confirmation that I would pass. I received the courage I needed that day to press through the gruesome three days of testing. I knew I would pass this time because I saw it.

After taking the bar exam for the second time, I waited four long months for the results. During that time, I continued working and serving. On November 18, 2016, I anxiously waited until 6 p.m. For the

140

first time since the first day of testing, my body was riddled with excitement and anxiety. I knew I had passed the exam this time. I was convinced I would become an attorney that day. I slowly typed in my credentials and waited for the screen to load. My stomach climbed to my throat for a few short seconds. When the screen turned, I read the information without blinking or breathing.

The red letters told me my name was not on the pass list. That's not what I wanted to see. I expected to see something different, so I told myself that I entered the numbers wrong. I re-entered my information several more times. Each time, the same message appeared. I could not believe it. I had not passed the bar exam again. I burst into tears.

The pain I experienced in that moment had been worse than all of the pain I had experienced in my life. I cried so hard that I could barely breath or see. I ran upstairs as fast I could and fell on my bedroom floor. My daughters walked in behind me with confused expressions on their little faces.

Aaliyah asked, "Mommy, what's wrong? You okay?"

I don't remember responding. They stood there staring at me as I fell apart until Aaliyah finally told Myah, "Let's go."

I continued to lay on the floor crying streams of hot tears. I couldn't understand how I had not passed the exam. I studied hard this time. I even implemented the techniques that got me through law school exams. My techniques *always* worked for me. I *always* scored high. I couldn't understand why they had not worked for me now. My scores were not reflecting the hard work and long hours I put into studying.

As my phone rang, I sent all phone calls except for one to voicemail. I was in a vulnerable state and I refused to allow anyone in except for Colbie. When I heard her voice on the other end of the phone, I blurted out the bad news. Even though I didn't want to talk, I needed someone to pull me out of my hysteria.

"It wasn't God's time for you to pass," Colbie replied.

I knew that was the case, but I didn't want to hear or believe it. After our short conversation, we hung up and I continued to cry.

The devastation I felt took me down a path of spiritual warfare. My thoughts started to become extremely negative. To make matters worse, I entertained them although I knew better. I started to feel hopeless. I became angry at life. I would cry out and ask God why He had not given me my heart's desire. I was serving Him like never before. I had continued to not date because he told me not to. I was living a life of abstinence. I was guarding my heart in every way possible. I was living a life truly surrendered unto Him! I just couldn't understand why I had not passed.

My warfare was extremely intense, and I stopped fighting. I stopped praying for a few days. I felt extreme numbness because of the pain. I had never been in that place before. I didn't know how I was going to get out of it. I knew I needed Jesus, but I was too upset to cry out to Him. I was fortunate I had praying women around me to pray me through. They were bold enough to speak the Lord's word over me. I was told I had to experience what I had been experiencing because of the women that would come behind me. They needed me to get through so that I could tell them how to go through devastation. After a week of feeling low, the tides turned and I was back to myself.

After the second failed attempt, I built enough courage to take the exam again. This time, everything seemed different. Instead of my paying the fees alone, I had family, friends, and co-workers sowing into me. God literally sent me the resources I needed. At first, I felt strange accepting the seeds until I was reminded of how much I encouraged other people. I was reminded that I needed to keep going because other people needed me. In that moment, I felt as though I wasn't alone. In that moment, I felt that I could do the impossible.

On the day of the exam, I walked into the testing center with a victorious attitude. I didn't feel defeated or overconfident. Instead I believed, regardless of the results, that I was taking another step towards the fulfillment of my dream. I knew God's will would prevail. As I waited for the results, I was prepared for whatever outcome. I knew my steps were ordered by the Lord. When I found out I had not passed again, I was hurt but not defeated. I knew that the Lord was still writing my story. I knew that what was happening was greater than me. I knew at the appointed time I would take the exam and pass it.

CHAPTER 22:CROSSING OVER

December 2016 was filled with a lot of adversity. My dreams started to center around my own life. I couldn't understand why, but I knew every dream I had been having was necessary. The dreams that stood out the most to me involved my ex. In the dreams, Maurice was always sitting quietly watching me. I would wake up praying and asking God why was he in my dreams. I wanted nothing to do with him. I didn't want to be with him. I made it a point to tell God these things, because I didn't want God to delay my husband finding me. One dream in particular stood out even more. As I gazed out of an open window, I saw a mountain far off. Behind the mountain were bright lights. As I stared at the mountain, light rain fell from the sky. I was mesmerized. When I turned around to my right, my ex was sitting on a couch staring at me. I looked at him and asked him why had he been there. He didn't answer me. I told him to look out the window, but he wouldn't move. I continued to look out of the window in complete awe until I woke up.

As I sat in my bed trying to wrap my mind around things, I started to pray. I repeatedly asked God why had Maurice suddenly appeared in my dreams.

The Lord told me, "because he is watching and waiting."

"Okay," I replied as I continued to wonder. He had not called my daughters in weeks and I didn't know why. He had just stopped communicating with them for some unknown reason. I was upset, but I held my peace.

One Monday morning as I sat at my work desk, I was led to visit Maurice's Facebook page. He and I were not friends, so I had to search for him. I didn't understand why I had such a strong urge to go to his page. I didn't question it. I knew that there was something I needed to see. After a few clicks, I understood why. My mouth instantly dropped. I came across a picture of beautiful little girl. As I looked into her eyes, I felt as though I was staring in the eyes of my baby girl Myah. That day, she was turning three years old. The little girl was his daughter.

I became sick to my stomach and grateful at the same time. My ex had another daughter who was seven months younger than the child we shared. He hid the fact he had another child from me for three entire years. He never mentioned her in any of the conversations we had when we were friends. I walked outside that morning and praised God because He had protected me. At the time the baby was conceived and born, I was still in a relationship with him. I now understood why God made me leave him. God knew what he was doing. God knew he wasn't the best for me. God refused to allow me to settle. I was grateful.

That day I saw what was on the other side of disobedience. Had I ignored God's instruction to leave him, I would have lost my mind. At that time, I was already depressed. Experiencing one more devastating event would have pushed me over the edge. I would have had to be institutionalized. I could not believe how much God loved me. I could not believe how concerned the Lord was with my heart and mind. I was extremely grateful for the Lord's protection. He allowed me to find out the ugly truth at a time when I was strong enough to handle it.

Exactly seven days after I found out about the baby girl, I sat at my desk at work checking my email. Suddenly, my phone started to buzz. I was a little surprised because it was only 8:36 a.m. I looked down at my phone and noticed I had a text message. I clicked on the message and was stunned. Maurice had gotten married that weekend to the woman he cheated on me with and had two babies with. My dream made a lot of sense in that moment. God was telling me to look to the hills because there was beauty on the other side. God knew what I was about to discover. He even told me he would marry her that Wednesday before they got married. I just didn't expect it would be that weekend.

I wasn't upset at all. I praised God for His protection. I praised God for His love, mercy, and grace. God could have left me in that situation. I could have ruined my life and married him. But God thought enough of me that He refused to allow me to settle. He refused to allow me to forfeit my destiny.

For the next few weeks, God continued to council me. I was tested at every turn. At times, I felt as if I wouldn't survive the warfare. I knew I couldn't do it on my own. I knew I had to hold on to God for dear life. I found myself praying a whole lot more. Anger would suddenly rise up within me. I would get the urge to lash out, but the Holy Spirit would talk me down. The Holy Spirit was my shield and the Lord was my strength.

When the warfare seemed to be at an all time high, I received a call to go on a fast. I had already felt that something was going on in the spirit realm. I just didn't know what. When my older cousin called me, I understood. He told me that God was trying to birth something inside of me. He told me I needed to go on a complete fast for three days. He confirmed everything I had felt in under five minutes.

I fasted for three long, hard days. I prayed during that time, asking God for guidance. I cried out for Him to birth whatever He wanted to birth out of me. My flesh was very weak during this fast. I was starving. I felt as if I would die. But in those moments, I would proclaim, "do it, Jesus!" until the urges and pain passed. I knew the fast was for a bigger purpose. I knew I needed to make it through so that I could see the beauty on the other side of the mountain.

My fast ended on December 31, 2016. That morning, God woke me up at 6 a.m. Immediately, He started to speak. I lay there astonished. The Lord revealed to me that He was calling me to form a LLC. He told me I would own a motivational speaking company that would host conferences. The Lord even gave me that name of my motivational speaking company. I couldn't believe my ears. I knew nothing about being a motivational speaker. I didn't even have a desire to do it. I knew nothing about forming or running a business. But I knew that if God said it, I could do it.

I continued to lay in bed amazed. I was full. I was grateful. I felt unworthy, but I knew I could do all things through Christ because He would equip me. Suddenly, He spoke again.

"You're writing a book. The title of the book is Confessions of An Overcomer: From Tragedy to Triumph." I was shocked. I had no desire to write anything. As I started to ask God for clarification, He told me to share my story as He leads me.

"My God," I thought, astonished. I never thought my story was special enough to share until that morning.

As the clock struck 12 a.m., I was relieved. I was over the mountain of 2016. My exit had been rough. My exit had been filled with many heart-wrenching tests. I had only survived because I held on to God. I praised the Lord that night because I knew I had crossed over into greatness. I praised God because I was walking into 2017 with clean hands. I had completely forgiven my mother. I had completely forgiven my father. I had completely forgiven my three molesters. I had completely forgiven all of my exes. I was only able to do it all because I held on to Jesus.

Walking with Jesus turned the tragedies of my life into triumphs. I overcame the spirit of suicide. I overcame the spirit of homosexuality. I overcame the spirit of fear. I overcame the spirit of rejection. I overcame the spirit of shame. I overcame everything the devil sent my way because through Christ, I am an overcomer.

CHAPTER 23: THE JOURNEY TO OVERCOMING

My journey towards overcoming required small and deliberant steps. During my process there were some great days and some not so great days. There were times when I wanted to give up and throw in the towel. While there were days when I felt like I could conquer the world. Regardless of how I felt I had to hold on to my belief that I would ultimately overcome.

When I was a small child my mother told me I could do whatever I wanted to do. She said all that was required was for me to work towards it. To this day I still rely on those same words to give me the strength I need to pursue my dreams. While I was going through difficult times these very words fueled the fire that lay in my belly. During my many trials and tribulations my mother's words helped me to push past my feelings towards the direction of overcoming.

To help me overcome I wrote down everything I believed I could accomplish. I kept, and still keep, journals, notebooks, and post-its close by. Whatever I wrote on I placed on walls, doors, in other notebooks, and anywhere else I could think of. Writing things down and placing them in different places played a vital role in me overcoming. These reminders helped me to stay motivated during the darkest hours of my life. It's as if every written word picked me up whenever I was down.

Aside from writing things down, I surrounded myself around positive influences. These individuals possessed the qualities I had buried inside of me. These individuals helped teach me how to be who

I was just by being who they were. They helped me remain positive at the weakest points in my life. And they helped to push me towards overcoming every obstacle in my path.

The biggest hurdle I encountered during my journey to overcome was learning to forgive those who hurt and betray me. No matter much I thought I had truly forgiven everyone, I was faced with the reality that I had not. True forgiveness did not take place until God spoke directly to me. That day as I drove home thinking about everything I had endured and overcome, the Lord uttered "broken people will do anything to make themselves feel whole. Even if it means hurting the people they love." Immediately after hearing these words something within me snapped. I had been molested because my abusers were broken. I wasn't protected because my mother was broken. I had been cheated on because my ex had been broken. I couldn't expect a broken person to do things someone who was healed and whole would do. They too would have to undergo their own process towards becoming an overcomer.

No matter what situation you find yourself faced with, you too can overcome. The faithfulness, protection, deliverance, healing, mercy, and grace God bestowed upon me, He'll do it for you too. God is not partial toward His children and His creation. He loves us all beyond measure. God desires for us all to overcome the trials and tribulations we encounter in this life. He sent his beloved son, Jesus, to die on the cross so that we will always overcome.